Teresa George

KEY CONCEPTS IN
Health and Social Care

John Rowe and Ann Mitchell

William Collins' dream of knowledge for all began with the publication of his first book in 1819. A self-educated mill worker, he not only enriched millions of lives, but also founded a flourishing publishing house. Today, staying true to this spirit, Collins books are packed with inspiration, innovation and practical expertise. They place you at the centre of a world of possibility and give you exactly what you need to explore it.

Collins. Freedom to teach

Published by Collins
An imprint of HarperCollins*Publishers*
77 – 85 Fulham Palace Road
Hammersmith
London
W6 8JB

Browse the complete Collins catalogue at
www.collins.co.uk

10 9 8 7 6 5 4 3 2 1

ISBN-13 978 0 00 751081 8

British Library Cataloguing in Publication Data
A Catalogue record for this publication is available from the British Library

Commissioned by Catharine Steers
Project managed by Sue Chapple
Production by Rebecca Evans

Typeset by Jouve India Private Limited
Proof read by Pat Dunn
Indexed by Jane Coulter
Photo research by Stephen Haskins
Concept design by Angela English
Cover design by Angela English

Printed and bound in China.

Acknowledgements
The publishers wish to thank the following for permission to reproduce photographs. Every effort has been made to trace copyright holders and to obtain their permission for the use of copyright material. The publishers will gladly receive any information enabling them to rectify any error or omission at the first opportunity.

p 4 tlorna/Shutterstock; p9 Thomas M Perkins/ Shutterstock; p.11 tommaso lizzul/Shutterstock; p 15 Lichtmeister/Shutterstock; p.17, 42, 88, 134, 167 Monkey Business Images/Shutterstock; p.23 Dundanim/Shutterstock; p.25 Prixel Creative/ Shutterstock; p28, 58 Rob Marmion/Shutterstock; p 31, 33 Stocklite/Shutterstock; p35 CREATISTA/ Shutterstock; p 39, 179 Goodluz/Shutterstock; p.44 Pixel Memoirs/Shutterstock; p 46, 63, 81, 158 Alexander Raths/Shutterstock; p 49 Kati Molin/ Shutterstock; p 51 Evgeniya Porechenskaya/ Shutterstock; p 61 Anetta/Shutterstock; p 67 digitalreflections/Shutterstock; p 69, 173 Marcel Jancovic/Shutterstock; p 73 Sam72/Shutterstock; p 77 Lisa S./Shutterstock; p 79, 112 Lisa F. Young/ Shutterstock; p.83 herjua/Shutterstock; p 86 Tsekhmister/Shutterstock; p 92 Stephen Griffith/ Shutterstock; p 94 Dmitry Berkut/Shutterstock; p97 gosphotodesign/Shutterstock; p.99, 169, 175 Yuri Arcurs/Shutterstock; p 104 peppi18/Shutterstock; p.108 filmfoto/Shutterstock; p.115 Lightspring/ Shutterstock; p 118 Vucicevic Milos/Shutterstock; p122 Jack.Q/Shutterstock; p 124 Digital Storm/Shutterstock; p.127 Tyler Olson/Shutterstock; p.129 JohnKwan/ Shutterstock; p.136 Kenneth William Caleno/ Shutterstock; p 143 ConstantinosZ/Shutterstock; p 145 PSD photography/Shutterstock; p.149 Steve Jacobs/ iStockphoto; p.156 Cartoonresource/Shutterstock; p.160 Orange Line Media/Shutterstock; p 162 berna namoglu/Shutterstock; p 181 iQoncept/Shutterstock; p188 Robert J. Daveant/Shutterstock; p192 Elnur/ Shutterstock

Contents

Abuse

The way people in care are treated has been the subject of much attention, with news media and policy-makers focusing on what is wrong. Often care workers are accused of mistreatment of the individuals they are paid to look after. In other instances, family members are reported to have been causing harm to their relative. These are examples of abuse.

What are the forms of abuse?

Abuse is mistreatment of or harm to another individual, whether a child or an adult. It can be deliberate harm, or any action or omission that leads to neglect and interferes with the individual's health, wellbeing or development. A situation where a person fails to act to prevent harm to another individual might also be seen as abuse; an example might be when one parent does not report or get help for a child who is being abused by the other parent. Abuse can happen regardless of age, gender, social class or ability, and occurs across all cultural and ethnic groups.

The Health and Social Care Information Centre (HSCIC, 2011) identifies the main forms of abuse as follows:

➤ Physical abuse may involve hitting, shaking, poisoning, burning, scalding, drowning or suffocating, or otherwise causing physical harm.

➤ Psychological and emotional abuse includes persistent emotional maltreatment, such as making a child feel worthless or unloved. Other examples are when an individual is used only to meet the needs of another person, or a child is overprotected and has limitations put on his or her activities. An abuser might also frighten or threaten another person.

➤ Financial abuse can lead to money being taken, bank accounts being mismanaged, wills being manipulated or property 'borrowed' or going missing.

➤ Neglect and omitting to take certain actions to protect an individual from harm is also a type of abuse. An example is persistent failure to meet an older person's basic needs such as adequate food and clothing, shelter or heating.

➤ Sexual abuse involves sexual activities that are against the individual's will, whether he or she is aware of or understands what is happening or not. It can also involve being made to watch or being exposed to sexual activity or images.

➤ Discriminatory abuse occurs when an individual is treated unfairly or differently because of his or her age, race, clothing, sexual orientation or disability.

➤ Institutional abuse occurs within an organisation such as a care home where a lack of concern by staff members means abusive behaviour comes to be regarded as normal. A culture of fear might mean abuse goes unchallenged, or the routines and procedures of the care service are carried out in ways that fail to acknowledge individual differences, needs and wishes.

Mowlam *et al* (2007) studied abuse in older people and found that their limiting circumstances mean that they cannot act to avoid abuse. They may have low self-confidence and esteem; they may be physically frail or not understand the seriousness of the mistreatment they experience. This can also be the case for many children and young people; those with special needs are also vulnerable.

Actions that workers in health and social care should take to avoid abuse are:

➤ Always be aware of the potential for abuse.

➤ If you are concerned that someone is being abused, share your concerns with a person in authority or in a designated safeguarding role, and/or with police or social services.

➤ Follow the safeguarding policy at your place of work.

➤ Don't fail to act on suspicions of abuse.

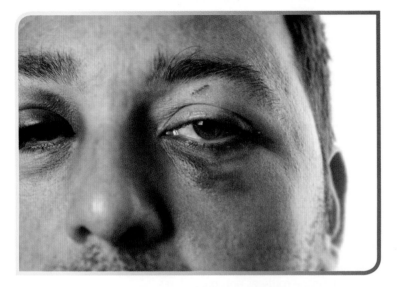

Summary

Abuse is harm caused to another person, whether a child or an adult. It can be physical, psychological, emotional, financial, sexual, discriminatory or institutional. It can also include neglect and omitting to do something. Health and social care workers have a role in tackling abuse, beginning with being aware that it can happen, and ensuring that if they suspect abuse they do something about it.

References

HSCIC (2011), *Abuse of Vulnerable Adults in England, 2010–11: Experimental statistics, Provisional report*, Health and Social Care Information Centre, Social Care Statistics

Mowlam, A., Tennant, R., Dixon, J. and McCreadie, C. (2007), *UK Study of Abuse and Neglect of Older People: Qualitative findings*, London, National Centre for Social Research

Accountability

A common phrase we hear is that someone should be 'held to account' for an action that has led to adverse consequences, or for actions not taken that lead to something going wrong. The idea applies particularly to health and care services where individuals' lives and wellbeing can be at stake. Service users should expect any care and treatment they receive to be beneficial to them and not to harm them. Care workers therefore are accountable for what they do and omit to do.

What is accountability?

Accountability means being responsible to someone, or for some action, and that you are able to explain what you do. Being accountable therefore involves being prepared to describe and justify (account for) your actions to others so that they can decide whether you have fulfilled what is expected of you. There is also the implication that if you do not fulfil your duties, either you or your employer will be held accountable; you or your employer may be penalised (Checkland *et al*, 2004).

Professionals in health and social care are held accountable for their work by their regulatory bodies. For example, social workers in England are obliged to comply with the General Social Care Council's guidance: they must be 'accountable for the quality of their work and take responsibility for maintaining and improving their knowledge and skills' (GSCC, 2010). Likewise, nurses are accountable to their professional body, which requires that they are 'personally accountable for actions and omissions' in their professional practice and must always be able to justify their decisions (NMC, 2008).

In addition to professional regulatory bodies, care workers are also accountable to:

➤ the people they look after and their families and carers, in ensuring care is safe and effective

➤ their employer, in ensuring they fulfil their duties and justify their decisions

➤ their colleagues, in ensuring they act in a responsible way

➤ themselves, in ensuring they uphold personal standards and maintain and improve their knowledge and skills.

Care workers can demonstrate accountability by:

➤ keeping records of what they do, including reasons for any omissions

➤ following guidelines and protocols

➤ providing safe and high quality care.

Summary

Accountability means being responsible to someone, or for some action, and ensuring that you are able to explain what you do. Care workers are accountable to their professional bodies, their clients, employers and colleagues, as well as themselves. They can demonstrate accountability by keeping records, following guidelines and working safely.

References

Checkland, K., Marshall, M. and Harrison, S. (2004), 'Re-thinking accountability: Trust versus confidence in medical practice', *Quality and Safety in Health Care*, 13 (2), 130–5

GSCC (2010), *Codes of Practice for Social Care Workers*, London, General Social Care Council

NMC (2008), *The Code: Standards of conduct, performance and ethics for nurses and midwives*, London, Nursing and Midwifery Council

Active participation

Increasingly, people who use health and social care services are becoming active participants in their own care. They are no longer the passive recipients of services. Through ensuring active participation, care services and care workers can empower individuals to attain a greater control over their lives.

What is active participation?

Active participation can be defined as recognising an individual's right to make decisions about and participate in the activities and relationships of everyday life as independently as possible. This means that the individual is an active partner in his or her own care and is not placed in a subordinate position to those who are providing care.

This definition supports the rights of individuals and their independence or autonomy. This is in keeping with the government's modernisation agenda for public services, which was enacted through legislation including the NHS Plan (DH, 2000). Modernisation is about involving the people who use services in the way services are delivered, and about focusing on individual users' needs and preferences rather than on what services and workers want to provide.

Upholding the personal autonomy of the individual is an important component of active participation. The Principles of Participation leaflet (GSCC *et al*, 2006) outlines how active participation can enhance individuals' autonomy, ensuring that individuals fully understand the reasons for the activities they participate in, and make informed choices about how they will be involved.

Active participation brings clear benefits for individuals. These can be divided into primary benefits and secondary benefits. Primary benefits include:

➤ physical benefits brought about by increased activity

➤ increased opportunities for social contact and interpersonal relationships

➤ greater involvement through awareness of opportunities

➤ fulfilling opportunities for learning and development of important skills, knowledge, education and employment

➤ enhanced wellbeing, self-confidence, self-esteem and self-belief.

The following secondary benefits also occur as a result of active participation:

➤ decreasing likelihood of abuse as individuals engage positively in areas of their lives such as personal care

➤ decreasing vulnerability to exploitation as individuals gain self-confidence and self-esteem.

Care workers can promote active participation by engaging individuals in their own care and in the way services are organised and delivered. It is important to ask individuals what they want to do and how they want to carry out an activity; to explain alternatives and choices they might have; to raise their awareness of different opportunities; and not to assume an individual cannot do something without good evidence that this is the case.

Summary

Active participation is an approach that empowers individuals in the activities and relationships of everyday life, enabling them to live as independently as possible. The importance for the individual as an active partner in his or her own care or support is that this brings physical, psychological, relational and overall benefits to wellbeing.

References

DH (2000), *The NHS Plan: A plan for investment, a plan for reform*, London, Department of Health

Edexcel (2011), *Edexcel Level 3 Diploma in Health and Social Care (Adults) for England (QCF)*, Harlow, Pearson Education

GSCC, CSCI, SfC and SCIE (2006), *Eight Principles for Involving Service Users and Carers*, General Social Care Council, Commission for Social Care Inspection, Skills for Care and Social Care Institute for Excellence

Activities of daily living

Most people take for granted, while going about their daily business, the ability to take care of their personal hygiene, their appearance and other everyday activities. However, for users of health and social care services, such activities cannot always be taken for granted. Activities of daily living (ADL) is a term and concept adapted by Roper, Logan and Tierney (1980).

What are activities of daily living?

Activities of daily living include the self-care activities people normally carry out in their day-to-day lives, such as washing, dressing, eating, moving and using the toilet. Ideas about ADL are founded on the work of Maslow (1943) who proposed patterns of human motivation. These are usually portrayed as a pyramid consisting of five layers representing physiological needs, safety, love and belonging, esteem and self-actualisation.

The concept of ADL is now used extensively in the UK. Each activity is linked to biological, social or psychological needs required for health (Kozier *et al*, 2008).

The activities concerned are:

➤ maintaining a safe environment

➤ communicating

➤ breathing

➤ eating and drinking

➤ eliminating

➤ personal cleansing and dressing

➤ controlling body temperature

➤ mobilising

➤ working and playing

➤ expressing sexuality

➤ sleeping

➤ dying.

This list is designed for care workers to use in assessing the ability of the service user or client to attend to his or her own needs. If deficits are identified, care workers can target interventions. For example, by assessing an individual with chronic obstructive pulmonary disease against each of the 12 elements, a care worker might identify that the individual has difficulties with breathing, mobilising and sleeping. In the community, the list is expanded to include the ability to shop, cook, manage money, and so on.

The list of activities of daily living has been criticised for not involving the individual in assessing his or her own needs, and for its tendency to focus on a medical model of care. Its use can seem limited to overcoming illness and disability, without taking sufficient account of an individual's holistic needs.

Summary

Activities of daily living are the self-care activities people normally carry out in their day-to-day lives, such as washing, dressing, eating, moving and using the toilet. The concept is used extensively in the UK in care settings as it lists elements that can be used to assess an individual's health status.

References

Kozier, B., Erb, G., Berman, A., Snyder, S., Lake, R. and Harvey, S. (2008), *Fundamentals of Nursing: Concepts, process and practice*, London, Pearson Education

Maslow, A.H. (1943), 'A theory of human motivation', *Psychological Review*, 50 (4), 370–96

Roper, N., Logan, W. and Tierney, A. (1980), *The Elements of Nursing*, Edinburgh, Churchill Livingstone

Advance decisions

Every day we make decisions, usually about small personal things, that help make our lives more comfortable or enable us to choose between different options: which shop to buy groceries from and which TV programme to watch, for example. Sometimes the decisions we make are more important, such as where we live and with whom.

Advance decisions, statements and directives

When people are aware that they might lose their ability to make decisions for themselves about everyday matters, perhaps because of a mental illness, dementia, or other illness or condition, it is important to let others know about their wishes for the future.

These preferences for the future fall into three types:

➤ advance decisions

➤ advance statements

➤ advance directives.

An advance decision is a way for individuals to say how they would like to be treated in the future if they ever lose the ability to decide for themselves. It is intended to be a binding refusal of certain kinds of treatment, as specified by the person making the advance decision (Alzheimer's Society, 2012).

The Mental Capacity Act (2005) allows for people to make decisions about their future. These decisions must be put into writing, signed by the person and witnessed.

➤ An advance decision directs who an individual would like to manage his or her practical matters if the individual becomes ill.

➤ There is a legal difference between statements that refuse treatment and statements that make requests.

➤ Only an advance decision to refuse treatment can be legally binding, but other statements should normally be followed by doctors (Rethink, 2011).

An advance statement is a statement of general beliefs and outlook on life. It may reflect individual aspirations and preferences. The advance statement can be used to help health professionals and others, such as family members, to decide what sort of treatment a person who is unable to communicate would want.

However, an advance statement would not commit health professionals to any particular course of action if it conflicted with their professional judgement (Alzheimer's Society, 2012).

An advance directive is also known as a living will. It expresses preferences about medical care, such as any refusal of treatment when an individual's condition deteriorates. To make an advance directive, the individual must be:

➤ competent at the time that the advance directive is declared

➤ informed about the procedure and what it involves

➤ free from the undue influence of others.

Advance directives that were made before the Mental Capacity Act (2005) have been replaced by advance decisions. If an individual has an advance directive, but has since lost mental capacity, it may still be valid and applicable under the Mental Health Act (Alzheimer's Society, 2012).

Summary

The law allows people to make decisions in advance about their future. These preferences for the future fall into three types: advance decisions, advance statements and advance directives.

References

Alzheimer's Society (2012), *Advance Decision*, London, Alzheimer's Society

Mental Capacity Act 2005 (c. 9), London, The Stationery Office

Rethink (2011), *Advance Statements: Planning for the future*, Factsheet, London, Rethink Mental Illness

Advocacy

A familiar position for many people when they come into contact with health and social care services is that they do not know what provision is available and what they can expect. Often this poor awareness of the availability of services is worse for particular groups and individuals in society. Advocacy is a means by which these difficulties can be overcome.

Using advocacy

Advocacy means supporting people to make informed choices about their care and treatment. It is about helping people to have a voice and speak for themselves, without influencing what they want to say. Action for Advocacy (undated) defines advocacy as:

> ❛taking action to help people say what they want, secure their rights, represent their interests and obtain services they need. Advocates and advocacy schemes work in partnership with the people they support and take their side. Advocacy promotes social inclusion, equality and social justice.❜

In health and social care, certain individuals and groups can benefit from advocacy because of their condition, illness or other circumstances. In particular the following can find a voice through advocacy:

➤ people with severe mental health problems

➤ individuals with learning disabilities

➤ young people who are in care or leaving local authority care

➤ people for whom there are language barriers to accessing services

➤ older people with communication problems.

Some people contend that all workers in health and social care should be advocates for the people in their care. The NMC (2008) states that nurses must act as advocates for those in their care, helping them to access relevant health and social care, information and support. However, this can potentially cause a conflict of interest, where care workers

advocate for the use of their own services. The use of independent advocacy services that are not employed by health and social care services may provide a wider perspective.

Summary

Advocacy means giving people a voice, so they can secure their rights, represent their interests and obtain services they need. It is particularly beneficial for individuals and groups who have difficulty communicating and with accessing services. Health and social care workers have a role in advocating for people in their care, but there is also a need for independent advocacy services.

References

Action for Advocacy (undated), 'About advocacy', http://www.actionforadvocacy.org.uk/articleServlet?action=list&articletype=10 (accessed 31 January 2013)

NMC (2008), *The Code: Standards of conduct, performance and ethics for nurses and midwives*, London, Nursing and Midwifery Council

Affirmative model

Often people with disabilities, especially disabilities that are evident to others, are assumed to be victims of personal tragic circumstances that are no fault of their own and therefore they deserve our pity. The affirmative model of disability is a 'non-tragic' view of disability and impairment. It is positive in outlook, both for individuals and groups of individuals, and based on the benefits of lifestyle and the experience of being impaired and disabled.

What is the affirmative model of disability?

The model grew out of the literature by disabled people and within disability culture, and has been expressed best by the Disability Arts Movement (Swain and French, 2000). Cameron (2008) clarified the meaning of disability and impairment so that they could be better understood within the affirmative model:

➤ Disability is the loss or limitation of opportunities to take part in community life on an equal level with others due to physical and social barriers.

➤ Impairment is the physical, sensory and intellectual difference to be expected and respected on its own terms in a diverse society.

The affirmative model of disability therefore focuses more on human difference than on any defect, and it directly challenges negative portrayals of disability. Detrich (2011) identifies advantages of the affirmative model: promise, potential, aspiration and dreams to be realised; people affirming a positive identity for themselves.

Summary

The affirmative model of disability is a 'non-tragic' view of disability and impairment. It is positive in outlook and based on the benefits of lifestyle and the experience of being impaired and disabled. The affirmative model of disability focuses more on human difference than on any defect and directly challenges negative portrayals of disability.

References

Cameron, C. (2008), 'Further towards an affirmation model' in Campbell, T., Fontes, F., Hemingway, L., Soorenian, A. and Till, C. (eds), *Disability Studies: Emerging insights and perspectives*, Leeds, Disability Press

Detrich (2011), 'Putting myself in the picture to evaluate the affirmative model of disability', Detrich's Weblog, 14 November 2011, http://detrich.wordpress.com/tag/affirmative-model-of-disability/ (accessed 31 January 2013)

Swain, J. and French, S. (2000), 'Towards an affirmation model of disability', *Disability and Society*, 15 (4), 569–82

Ageing

When individuals enter health and social care, one of the first details we seek about them is how long they have been alive. We record their date of birth and age. In short, we measure their age in chronological terms marked by annual birthdays. However, the length of time a person has been alive is only one way in which an individual's age can be described.

What are the types of ageing?

The World Health Organization sees ageing as 'a privilege and a societal achievement', while also a challenge to 21st-century society (WHO, 2012). There is not a uniform pattern for people to follow as they age. While knowing someone's chronological age helps care workers to assess what services can best meet the needs of the individual, different factors affect the ageing process. These factors affect the types of ageing and can act singly or in combination with each other.

Apart from chronological ageing, DiGiovanna (2000) also identifies other types of ageing:

➤ **Biological ageing**: An individual's potential lifespan, that is the time he or she has to live, is affected by biological ageing. Biological ageing can often dominate care workers' and others' views on the ageing process. There tends to be an emphasis on illness and reduced abilities to perform activities of daily living as people grow older. The important thing to understand is that an individual's biological age can be different from his or her chronological age, so that a 94-year-old woman might still be lively and alert while a 34-year-old man might be hospitalised with a terminal condition.

➤ **Psychological ageing**: Psychological ageing relates to the mental ability to adapt to changing circumstances in order to achieve goals. A person who is confident and has high self-esteem will age psychologically at a different rate from an individual who lacks motivation, has declining mental capacity and is emotionally distressed.

➤ **Social ageing**: People of a particular chronological age are usually expected to fulfil certain roles and behave in ways particular to their culture. In the UK today most older people have retired from paid work; however, this is not always the case, as older people now work longer.

➤ **Economic ageing**: This refers to age-related changes in the economic status of individuals. They might have accumulated wealth or live on benefits.

➤ **Cosmetic ageing**: This refers to changes in appearance due to biological ageing or other factors.

Summary

There are different types of ageing: chronological, biological, psychological, social, economic and cosmetic. These can be alternative ways of describing the ageing process and can act either singly or in combination with each other.

References

DiGiovanna, A.G. (2000), *Human Aging: Biological perspectives*, New York, McGraw-Hill

WHO (2012), 'Types of healthy settings: Healthy ageing', World Health Organization, http://www.who.int/healthy_settings/types/ageing/en/index.html/ (accessed 31 January 2013)

Ageism

Any critical discussion of ageing and older people in Western society can easily lead to the issue of ageism. It is considered flattering to say to another person 'you don't look your age'. The undercurrent to such seemingly harmless statements is that it is not desirable to look or act old.

What is ageism?

We are faced with a new challenge as the population ages: the term 'demographic time-bomb' implies that society cannot afford to have too many older people using all the public services, taking retirement pensions and demanding suitable housing.

Ageism is a type of discrimination where people are treated differently because of that one characteristic: their age. They are treated differently because they are the older third of the population. Unlike race or gender, which is generally fixed at birth, age is a continuum – continuous sequence – (Age UK, 2011). It is therefore a form of discrimination that people approach and grow into as they become older. It is also the most prevalent form of discrimination in the UK today.

A report (Age UK, 2011) shows that in Europe most people believe that you become old at about the age of 62, and in the UK most people surveyed perceive old age starting at the age of 59. This is important for very practical reasons; the insurance industry, for example, may raise policy prices for older drivers, and employers might feel it is acceptable to make older workers redundant.

These types of discrimination are not the only examples of ageist attitudes and prejudice that older people encounter. Older people who experience ageist attitudes from others feel:

➤ patronised – this is often accompanied by assumptions that older people cannot do things, are in many ways incapable, and can be referred to with terms such as 'old dear'

➤ ignored – many older people feel invisible in today's culture where youth and looks are celebrated

➤ disrespected – there is a subtle prejudice against being old; the rapid growth of online services and mobile devices is an example of technology being aimed directly at younger people.

Ageism can have two effects on older people that reinforce cultural stereotypes:

1. They can see themselves as others see them: they might begin to think that they are unfairly using society's resources. They come to feel useless and a drain on younger generations.

2. They can lack self-respect, and accept patronising attitudes and being treated as invisible.

Summary

Ageism is a type of discrimination where people are treated differently because of their age. Ageist attitudes that patronise, ignore and disrespect older people are grounded in a society that perceives older age negatively, as undesirable and a drain on the country's resources.

References

Age UK (2011), *A Snapshot of Ageism in the UK and Across Europe*, London, Age UK

Agreed ways of working

When workers begin practising in health and social care settings, they are often worried about what they should do and how they should do it. However, there are guidelines that tell workers what to do in certain situations they may encounter. These guidelines are set out in policies and procedures, which workers are expected to follow as part of their contract of employment.

Policies and procedures

An agreed way of working is a policy or procedure in your workplace that you must abide by (OPPS, 2012). Policies are provided by the employer, and offer a general approach to dealing with issues in care. For example, there might be a policy on moving and positioning individuals stating that care workers should not lift individuals manually (by hand).

Procedures, on the other hand, provide a more detailed approach. Along with the policy on no manual lifting, there might be a procedure that outlines how lifting aids and equipment are to be used.

Health and social care settings are likely to have policies and procedures on most of the following:

➤ fire and other emergencies

➤ health and safety

➤ confidentiality

➤ data protection

➤ medication management

➤ equal opportunities

➤ moving and positioning individuals

➤ risk management.

There are likely to be other policies and procedures that are specific to each particular care setting: visiting hours, perhaps.

Many policies and procedures reflect legal requirements, but other organisations also influence policy development. These include charities and pressure groups, the National Institute for Health and Clinical Excellence, and professional bodies such as the Royal College of Nursing.

Individuals who use services are now more likely to contribute to policy development; this is to ensure that policies and procedures focus on what the people who use services want, and not what the service providers think is important.

Summary

An agreed way of working is a policy or procedure in a workplace that must be followed. Policies offer a general approach to what care workers are expected to do, while procedures outline particular instructions in more detail.

References

OPPS (2012), 'What are agreed ways of working?', OPPS Developments, http://www.oppsdevelopments.co.uk/blog/2012/07/question-what-are-agreed-ways-of-working/ (accessed 31 January 2013)

Assessment

Imagine going into a shoe shop to buy a new pair of boots for hill walking, and being greeted by a shop worker who supplies you with a pair of beach sandals. You would not expect this to happen; you would expect some sort of assessment of your needs and preferences and then to be offered a selection of walking boots. Similarly, health and social care services must make an assessment of individuals' needs and preferences. It is how they begin to meet individuals' requirements.

What is assessment?

Assessment involves gathering and analysing information about people with the aim of understanding their situation and determining recommendations for further intervention (Crisp *et al*, 2003). It is important in any care setting; without an assessment, care is unlikely to meet individuals' needs.

According to Whittington (2007), there are five purposes to assessment:

➤ to protect the individual and the public

➤ to identify the needs of service users and carers

➤ to represent or advocate for the service user or carer

➤ to act on an agency's policies or priorities

➤ to inform other agencies or professionals.

Assessment might be in response to government policy; for example, to protect vulnerable children and adults, or to integrate socially excluded people into society. These policies require an assessment of individuals' needs, which is reflected in the resources made available to meet any need.

Assessment can also be seen as a range of activities that have specific forms:

➤ Resource-led assessment means using the assessment process to ration resources or disguise their absence. A service will offer a particular intervention or range of care interventions, and individuals accept the care even if it does not meet their needs.

➤ Needs-led assessment is based on a diagnosis of the individual's situation, and is not determined by what is available but by what the person requires in terms of support and care. It can focus on individuals' strengths and what they can do, and not just on their deficits.

➤ A person-centred approach requires that the individual's views are given paramount importance in the assessment, and decisions made are a shared responsibility with the individual. This has been encapsulated in the phrase 'No decisions about me, without me' (Coulter and Collins, 2011).

➤ The Single Assessment Process (SAP) is an assessment tool that aims to ensure older people are treated as individuals and they receive care that meets their needs.

➤ An Overview Single Assessment is carried out in accordance with a government table of risk and need, the Fair Access to Care Services (FACS) framework, which has four eligibility levels: low, moderate, substantial and critical.

➤ Risk assessment is the determination of the possibility of accident or danger in relation to a given situation or any existing, recognised threat.

Summary

Assessment involves gathering and analysing information about people in order to understand their situation and determine any further intervention. It has a range of purposes and might be in response to government policy. It also takes different forms depending on the situation.

References

Coulter, A. and Collins, A. (2011), *Making Shared Decision-Making a Reality: No decision about me, without me*, London, King's Fund

Crisp, B.R., Anderson, M.T., Orme, J. and Green Lister, P. (2003), *Knowledge Review 1: Learning and Teaching in Social Work Education: Assessment*, London, Social Care Institute for Excellence

Whittington, C. (2007), *Assessment in Social Work: A guide for learning and teaching*, London, Social Care Institute for Excellence

Attachment theory

Human beings are social animals who form attachments to one another. Some attachments are strong: to family and friends, perhaps. Others are not so strong, perhaps to work colleagues. Babies form attachments with their parents or carers at a very early stage as they begin to explore the world. It is a special emotional relationship. Bowlby (1969) noted that babies interact with others by smiling and making noises. He rejected the view that babies were passive, just lying there looking at faces around them.

The characteristics and importance of attachment

Bowlby described attachment as a 'lasting psychological connectedness between human beings' (Bowlby,1969, p. 194). He believed that the bonds children form with those who care for them are vitally important for the individual as they influence development and behaviour throughout his or her life.

The core theme of attachment theory is that mothers or carers who are responsive to the infant's needs help the child to establish a sense of security. This enables the infant to feel safe as he or she begins to explore the world.

Bowlby believed that there are four main characteristics to attachment:

➤ proximity maintenance – the need to be near people we are attached to

➤ safe haven – returning to the attachment carer for safety when facing a threat

➤ secure base – attachment figures give security to children so that they can explore their immediate environment

➤ separation distress – the child develops anxiety when the attachment person is not present.

Ainsworth *et al* (1978) expanded on Bowlby's original work, revealing the effect attachment can have on behaviour. They discovered individual differences when observing mothers. Securely attached babies cried little and seemed content to explore in the presence of their mother, whereas insecurely attached babies cried frequently even when they were held by their mothers. Attachment relationships can vary from secure to insecure, and depend on the skills of the mother or carer.

Failure to form secure attachments can have a negative impact on behaviour in childhood and later life. These include conduct disorders such as being:

➤ indiscriminately affectionate with strangers

➤ destructive to self and others

➤ cruel to animals

➤ unable to give or receive affection

➤ inappropriately demanding or clingy.

Children need support in order to:

➤ be able to respond to a significant other and feel valued

➤ have a realistic sense of self

➤ accept responsibility for their own actions

➤ manage their feelings appropriately

➤ comply with basic rules of society (OAASIS, undated).

Summary

A baby will form attachment within the early months of life with the mother or another significant carer. Attachments are vitally important as they give emotional security throughout life. Bowlby has contributed much to the study on attachment that has helped us to understand the ways in which failure to form those early relationships can affect us during childhood and in later life.

References

Ainsworth, M., Blehar, M., Waters, E. and Wall, S. (1978), *Patterns of Attachment*, Hillsdale, Erlbaum

Bowlby, J. (1969), *Attachment and Loss, Vol. 1: Attachment*, New York, Basic Books

OAASIS (undated), 'Attachment disorder', Office for Advice, Assistance, Support and Information on Special Needs, http://www.oaasis.co.uk/ (accessed 31 January 2013)

Best interests

Person-centred practice demands that individuals are always involved in making the decisions that affect them directly. However, it is necessary sometimes to make decisions on other people's behalf because they lack the mental capacity to decide for themselves what action is in their best interests.

What is meant by the best interests of a person?

Acting in the best interests of a person is sanctioned under Principle 4 of the Mental Capacity Act (2005). Circumstances that might lead to invoking the Act include dementia, a severe stroke, a brain injury, a mental health problem, or a learning disability. If a person has been assessed as lacking capacity, any action taken, or any decision made for or on behalf of that person, must be made in his or her best interests (SCIE, undated).

Working for someone's best interests, of course, should always be paramount in health and social care. However, when it is considered necessary, legal support can be provided to overrule another person's decision or to make a decision on someone's behalf.

Before using the Mental Capacity Act to decide in another person's best interest, factors such as those in the following non-exhaustive list must be taken into account:

➤ Consider all the circumstances, especially whether the individual is likely to regain the capacity to make decisions.

➤ Encourage participation of the individual.

➤ Consult other people close to the individual.

➤ Consider the individual's past and present wishes.

➤ Avoid discrimination and making assumptions about what the person would prefer.

Summary

Principle 4 of the Mental Capacity Act allows others to decide in the best interests of individuals when they lack the mental capacity to make decisions for themselves. In doing so, many criteria must be taken into account.

References

Mental Capacity Act 2005 (c. 9), London, The Stationery Office

SCIE (undated), 'MCA resource: Five principles of the MCA', Social Care Institute for Excellence, http://www.scie.org.uk/publications/mca/principles.asp/ (accessed 31 January 2013)

Boundaries

When thinking about boundaries, most people think of the boundaries between neighbouring houses or borders between countries. However, it is important that workers in health and social care consider the boundaries around their role, their communication with colleagues, and their work with the people they care for.

What is a boundary?

For Parkes and Jukes (2008), a boundary is a professional rule of thumb, a marker or a limit. There are boundaries in all aspects of people's lives, but they have specific relevance to care. Workers need to be aware of boundaries in respect of professional roles, personal and interagency boundaries.

➤ **Professional relationships**: It is a requirement of professional regulatory bodies such as the Nursing and Midwifery Council (NMC) and the Social Care Council that nurses and social care workers develop and maintain professional relationships with others. The NMC (2008), for example, stipulates that nurses and midwives should maintain clear professional boundaries that include not accepting gifts, favours or loans, and keeping clear sexual boundaries with those they care for, their families and carers.

➤ **Personal boundaries**: As a care worker you might find yourself in the position of having to negotiate personal boundaries with the individual you are caring for. Receiving intimate care, such as being assisted to use the toilet, bathe or get dressed, can be embarrassing for both the carer and the person receiving care. This is because such care crosses the boundaries of normal social interaction.

➤ **Interagency boundaries**: Organisations and agencies in health and social care work with each other to ensure optimum care for individuals. Interagency working across organisational boundaries might be at individual level between two or more practitioners, or at organisational level through the exchange of contracts to provide and pay for services.

Summary

Boundaries in health and social care are rules that relate to professional relationships, the provision of intimate care that crosses normal social boundaries, and interagency working across different organisations.

References

NMC (2008), *The Code: Standards of conduct, performance and ethics for nurses and midwives*, London, Nursing and Midwifery Council

Parkes, N. and Jukes, M. (2008), 'Professional boundaries in a person-centred paradigm', *British Journal of Nursing*, 17 (21), 1358–64

Care planning

Every individual who enters into health and social care should have a care plan that details his or her care needs and preferences, how these needs and preferences can be met, and who is to be involved in meeting any needs. There are no exceptions to this rule. Without a care plan individuals will not receive the care they require, putting them and others at risk. Care planning is therefore an essential component of safe and effective care.

What are care plans?

Care plans set out how a package of support works, and are often called support plans (NHS Choices, 2012). Care or support plans assist in a person-centred approach to care. It is vital, in order for this to happen, that the individual the care plan is designed to support is involved in agreeing its content. The individual should also be given a copy of the plan.

Every care plan should contain information on the following:

➤ the individual's assessed needs

➤ the individual's circumstances and current support

➤ what both the care worker and the individual think are the desired outcomes of care

➤ any support or intervention that is required

➤ the timescale for implementing support.

However, to be truly person-centred the care plan should also contain information that outlines:

➤ the individual's strengths, interests and preferences

➤ how the individual likes to lead his or her life

➤ details of other people who are important to the individual.

In addition to the criteria set out above on what a care plan should contain, the Alzheimer's Society (2012) lists further information that should be included in a care plan for an individual with dementia:

➤ a risk assessment that outlines any dangers the individuals and others close to them might be in

➤ a plan for dealing with emergency changes, as sometimes individuals with Alzheimer's disease can do unexpected things

➤ the result of the financial assessment, as availability of care provision is means-tested

➤ the support that carers are willing and able to provide, with many informal carers experiencing health problems themselves.

Not all care plans use the same format, or means of recording. Many care plans are paper-based, but increasingly care plans are recorded using electronic methods. However, whatever format they are recorded in, they should always be reviewed regularly as individuals' needs or circumstances change.

Summary

Care plans or support plans set out how a package of support works. They contain essential information about the individual and his or her needs. To be person-centred they should also include information on the person's strengths and preferences. Care plans are available in different formats and should always be reviewed regularly to reflect individuals' changing needs and circumstances.

References

Alzheimer's Society (2012), *Community Care Assessment*, London, Alzheimer's Society

NHS Choices (2012), 'Care plan', http://www.nhs.uk/CarersDirect/guide/assessments/Pages/Thecareplan.aspx/ (accessed 31 January 2013)

Carers

It is estimated by Carers UK (2009) that there are six million informal carers in the UK; that is, one person in every eight has someone he or she provides care to. Most carers (58 per cent) are women, while men (42 per cent) also share this role. Over a million people care for more than one person – perhaps a mother and father.

What do carers do?

The term used for this army of carers varies, but they are most commonly described as informal carers. This term applies to caregivers who provide care to a family member or to others, a friend or neighbour perhaps. Caring is not usually limited to a few simple tasks. It can range from helping with the shopping on a regular basis to providing continuous care.

The key findings of the Office of National Statistics (2010) are that:

➤ women were more likely to care than men

➤ over half of all carers provided up to 19 hours of care per week, and just over one fifth provided round-the-clock care (168 hours)

➤ men were more likely than women to care for up to 19 hours, and less likely to care for between 20 and 49 hours

➤ men and women were equally likely to care round-the-clock

➤ women were more likely than men to care in older age, more likely to care for longer hours, and more likely to care for all categories of care recipients except for spouses/partners

➤ more than three quarters of carers were married, and two fifths of all carers lived with the person receiving care

➤ carers appeared to be more likely than non-carers to report good health and not to report a limiting longstanding illness, but health status deteriorated as care intensity rose.

Rowe (2012) found that family carers in mental health had expectations placed upon them. Caring for a family member was a distinctive role that most people were unprepared for. However, there are ways in which carers can provide effective care; they can, for instance, share information with care workers and get involved with packages of care. There are, though, barriers to effective caring. These barriers include carers being seen as troublemakers, not being listened to and feeling isolated. Fortunately barriers to effective care can be overcome through actions taken by care workers.

There are a number of simple steps care workers can take that will help support informal carers:

➤ Take account of an individual carer's rights and responsibilities.

➤ Have a positive and understanding attitude to the difficult role many informal carers perform.

➤ Include carers in treatment approaches by being approachable.

➤ Find out about the person's condition and his or her needs.

➤ Find out about any particular cultural issues that might affect care.

Summary

It is estimated there are six million informal carers in the UK who provide care to a friend or relative. For many it is a full-time role: providing personal care, practical assistance and supporting other care and treatment. Care workers can help support informal carers by taking account of individual carers' rights, being understanding of the difficult role many carry out, and finding out what particular support carers might require when providing effective care to their relative or friend.

References

Carers UK (2009), *Policy Briefing: Facts about carers*, London, Carers UK

ONS (2010), 'The demographic characteristics and economic activity patterns of carers over 50: Evidence from the English Longitudinal Study of Ageing', *Population Trends*, highlighted, 141, Office for National Statistics

Rowe, J. (2012), 'Great Expectations: A systematic review of the literature on the role of family carers in severe mental illness, and their relationship and engagement with professionals', *Journal of Psychiatric and Mental Health Nursing*, 19 (1), 70–82

Challenging behaviour

On occasions, individuals can exhibit behaviour that other people – including care workers – find difficult. Individuals might be disruptive, aggressive or violent, abusive, unsafe or behave in a socially inappropriate way. However, it should be borne in mind that the way that behaviour is described affects the way care workers try to respond to it. A generic term has been adopted to manage these types of undesirable behaviours more effectively: challenging behaviour.

What is challenging behaviour?

Lowe and Felce (1995) coined the expression 'challenging behaviour'. The term 'challenging behaviour' focuses on the behaviour rather than labelling the person as difficult. It implies the following:

➤ Responsibility for difficult behaviour is shifted from the service user to the care providers. The advantage of this is that the responsibility falls to care teams to account for and manage disruptive, aggressive, abusive or other forms of unsafe behaviour. The nature of the challenge is a shared responsibility with a greater requirement for care teams to understand and help the individual.

➤ In doing so, care teams can work out what the function of the undesirable behaviour is. This introduces the question: What does the individual achieve by behaving in that manner? So, instead of punitive measures (punishment), care teams can adapt care plans to help individuals to develop and maintain appropriate skills so that they can achieve their aims in a less disruptive and a safer way.

➤ The term 'challenging behaviour' lends itself more closely to a respectful and a less problem-orientated use of language, and one that is more in step with the person-centred approach to care.

Summary

The way behaviour is described affects the way care workers respond to it. The expression 'challenging behaviour' brings with it a number of associations that support a mutual (shared) responsibility between the carer and individual to manage behaviour in a more respectful and understanding way.

References

Lowe, K. and Felce, D. (1995), 'The definition of challenging behaviour in practice', *British Journal of Learning Disabilities*, 23 (3), 118–23

Child protection

The young are viewed as particularly vulnerable, and in a complex society like that of the UK today, protecting children from risk is a priority. Statutory guidance aims to help protect children and young people from harm, neglect and abuse. The terms 'child protection' and 'safeguarding children' are routinely used wherever children access health and social care services.

What are child protection and safeguarding?

Child protection and safeguarding are terms that are linked to each other. Safeguarding extends the idea of child protection to include the promotion of health and wellbeing; it fosters a culture where children are valued and their rights are respected. Risks should be minimised so that individuals feel safe in an environment where they can live and play (NSPCC, 2011).

Safeguarding is covered by the Children Act (2004), which is government legislation that aims to ensure children, young people and vulnerable adults are kept safe and free from harm.

Every Child Matters: Change for children (Department for Education and Skills, 2004) sets out a national framework for 150 local programmes of change to be led by English local authorities and their partners to enable this change. The main focus areas are early intervention, a shared sense of responsibility, information sharing and integrated front-line services. There are specific guidelines that all agencies must adhere to in order to proactively safeguard and promote the welfare of children.

Agencies must:

➤ take immediate action when they recognise that a child might be at risk of harm or abuse

- protect every child and young person from violence, abuse, bullying and discrimination

- prevent any damage or impairment that may affect the individual child's health and wellbeing

- ensure that children have a right to grow up in a safe and caring environment and to participate in the society in which they live

- raise concerns when appropriate, and make contact with the relevant emergency service.

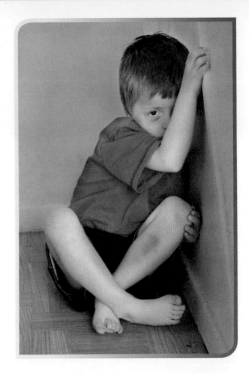

Summary

Child protection and safeguarding is enshrined in legislation that shields the individual child or young person from harm and abuse, and every effort should be made by the relevant agencies and bodies to contact appropriate services when concerns are recognised or raised.

References

Children Act 2004 (c. 31), London, The Stationery Office

Department for Education and Skills (2004), *Every Child Matters: Change for children*, London, The Stationery Office

NSPCC (2011), 'Safeguarding', http://www.safenetwork.org.uk/Pages/default.aspx (accessed 31 January 2013)

Communication

A key skill for workers in health and social care is the ability to communicate. Without good communication skills, individuals and their relatives will not be able to understand the care that is offered. This is particularly relevant for individuals who have a sensory loss, older people with dementia, and clients with a learning disability.

What is communication in care practice?

The General Social Care Council (GSCC, 2010) requires practitioners to communicate in an appropriate, open, accurate and straightforward way. This has implications for the way that care workers use communication, meaning that they must take into account the diverse range of individuals' communication needs, and their ill-health or impairing conditions.

Care workers need to know how to make, maintain and end relationships as they work with individuals who enter, continue to be supported by, and finally leave care services. In doing so, it is important to remember the following:

➤ Good communication is as much about listening as it is about talking. Messages are given and they are also received.

➤ Communication is both verbal and non-verbal. Body language such as gestures, positioning, eye contact, facial expressions and touch send more messages than words do.

➤ Care workers communicate with individuals and their families, but also with colleagues and other professionals.

➤ Care workers communicate in writing and electronically, as well as verbally and non-verbally.

Communication is recognised as an essential human need and therefore is a basic human right (R. Chris, 2011). To uphold this right, care workers can develop good communication techniques that are more than just informing individuals what they are going to do.

Good communication can be achieved with individuals by:

➤ being respectful – so that individuals are more likely to want communication with you

➤ establishing rapport – so that communication is easier and more effective

➤ giving time – individuals need time to understand the message you are sending and you need time to understand the message they send to you

➤ acting in an appropriate and professional manner – individuals in health and social care expect and deserve a high standard of communication

➤ adapting – to individuals' needs such as sensory loss or learning disability

➤ maintaining confidentiality – conveying personal and sensitive information on a need-to-know basis and in a private area.

Summary

Care workers must communicate in an appropriate, open, accurate and straightforward way, enabling them to make, maintain and end relationships with individuals who enter, continue to be supported by, and finally leave care services. Good communication can be achieved by being respectful and professional while adapting communication methods to the needs of the individual.

References

GSCC (2010), *Codes of Practice for Social Care Workers*, London, General Social Care Council

R., Chris (2011), 'Communication, or lack of communication', Personal blog, Rethink Mental Illness, 24 May 2011, http://www.rethink.org/about_mental_illness/personal_stories_blogs_forum/blogs/chris_r/communication_or_la.html/ (accessed 31 January 2013)

Conception

Many women and their partners perceive having a baby as an exciting time. Conception brings a change in the parents' lives and is often seen as a transition to a period of greater responsibility. To increase the chances of conception, lifestyle changes can be needed.

What is conception?

Conception can be defined in two terms. The first is when the ovum fuses with the sperm, which leads to the development of the foetus; that is, creating a new life. The second way conception can be understood is a bit simpler: it is the act of becoming pregnant (*Blackwell's Dictionary of Nursing*, 1994).

Conception does not happen immediately during or after sexual intercourse. The fastest a sperm can get to a Fallopian tube is about 30 minutes, meaning that the earliest conception can occur following sexual intercourse is about half an hour. But it may take five days or longer to conceive (Sheve, 2012).

There are several factors that can affect conception, including the following:

➤ **Age**: The woman's age is critical; post-menopausal women will require fertility treatment to conceive successfully.

➤ **Timing and frequency**: Sexual intercourse needs to be synchronised with the woman's ovulation.

➤ **Lifestyle factors**: Smoking in particular can be harmful to both male and female fertility, while excessive alcohol can impair male and female fertility.

➤ **Nutrition**: Adequate nutrition from a healthy balanced diet can aid conception.

➤ **Health**: Certain illnesses and medical conditions can affect fertility.

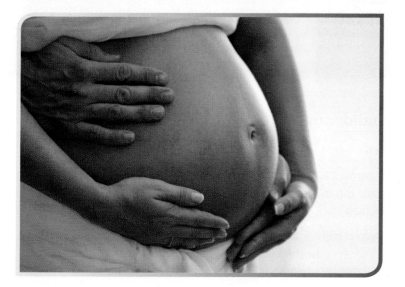

Summary

Conception is the act of becoming pregnant, and occurs when the ovum fuses with the sperm leading to the creation of a new life. Individuals need to be aware that when they and their partner are trying to conceive, they must prepare their bodies for this normal and natural event and avoid certain lifestyle factors that could prevent conception from occurring.

References

Blackwell's Dictionary of Nursing (1994), 'Conception', Oxford, Blackwell Science

Sheve, T. (2012), 'How long after sex does conception occur?', Discovery Communications, http://health.howstuffworks.com/pregnancy-and-parenting/pregnancy/conception/how-long-after-sex-does-conception-occur2.htm/ (accessed 31 January 2013)

Confidentiality

You wouldn't expect a stranger to know about your personal business. Similarly there are boundaries around who should know information about individuals who use health and care services. A key element of safe practice in health and social care is maintaining confidentiality. This does not mean that information about individuals should be kept secret, but that there are limits placed on sharing certain information; it should only be disclosed in order to support individuals on a 'need-to-know' basis.

What is confidentiality?

Confidentiality is:

➤ a legal requirement – the Data Protection Act (1998) guards against the misuse of personal information about individuals

➤ an ethical requirement – there is no reason why a person not concerned with an individual's care should have access to information about him or her

➤ a professional responsibility – social care workers, for example, must respect confidential information and clearly explain policies on confidentiality to individuals and their carers (GSCC, 2010).

However, the rules on confidentiality can be breached in some circumstances. These include:

➤ to protect an individual who is at risk of harm

➤ to prevent a crime being committed

➤ to help a child-abuse investigation

➤ if a court orders the disclosure of information.

Workers must comply with the agreed ways of working in their care setting. Information governance rules can help decide whether information can be disclosed, when issues arise about who can be told certain information. There is a particular problem where an individual is being looked after by a family member or other informal carer, but does not want this person to know personal information. In such situations the individual's care can be affected (Rowe, 2010). When this happens, care workers should seek advice about what information should or should not be disclosed.

Summary

Maintaining confidentiality is a legal, ethical and professional requirement that care workers must uphold. However, there are occasions when confidentiality can be breached. Care workers should seek advice on such occasions before they disclose personal information.

References

Data Protection Act 1998 (c. 29), London, The Stationery Office

GSCC (2010), *Codes of Practice for Social Care Workers*, London, General Social Care Council

Rowe, J. (2010), 'Information disclosure to family caregivers: Applying Thiroux's framework', *Nursing Ethics*, 17 (4), 435–44

Consent

In the normal course of life, few people would agree that anyone can touch or do things to another person without that person's permission. There are some exceptions, such as a baby's nappy being changed or an unconscious victim of a car accident being moved from a vehicle. But just because individuals use care services does not mean that they lose their right to decide who touches or does things for them. They are entitled to have their autonomy respected and their permission requested.

Establishing consent

Consent is a cornerstone of health and social care. In most circumstances, care workers are acting illegally unless they establish consent with individuals. Consent is giving permission to do something (*Collins Concise English Dictionary*, 2008). It is a legal requirement for carers to establish the consent of the person they are looking after before they carry out any care activity. In health and social care settings this usually means that the individual gives consent to take part in an activity or to accept some kind of care or treatment.

It is important to remember that:

➤ it is a legal requirement that consent is established before any intervention or care-giving activity takes place

➤ establishing consent is one way that care workers can demonstrate they respect the individual and the individual's personal dignity

➤ the process of establishing consent is instrumental to developing trust between the care worker and the individual

➤ the individual is more likely to want to take part in an activity he or she has given permission for.

Individuals can give consent in a number of ways. It is not always about signing a piece of paper or a legal document. Consent can be given verbally, in writing or through actions. Individuals might show that they allow another person to do something with or to them by actions such as raising an arm to be supported when dressing, thereby implying consent.

It is not sufficient to ask an individual if he or she agrees that you may carry out a care activity. It is important that the individual understands what the care is, why it is being carried out, any alternatives or choices that might be available, and any consequences of the care being carried out. Informed consent is given when the individual understands what he or she is consenting to. Indeed, the validity of informed consent can be questioned if the individual has not been given the opportunity to review all feasible options and express preferences (Coulter and Collins, 2011).

However, it is not always possible to establish informed consent, and in some circumstances the individual might withhold consent. Individuals might withhold permission for an action to be performed because care workers:

➤ do not understand the individual's needs, condition or capacity to make decisions

➤ do not have the relevant information or are unable to impart the information in a form that is understandable by the individual

➤ do not themselves understand the options that are available, and any potential or actual risks to the individual.

There are, however, some things that care workers can do to try to gain consent when it is withheld by an individual in their care. Care workers can:

➤ ensure they understand and act on understanding of the individual's health status or condition and ability to make decisions

➤ ensure they understand the individual's needs and preferences and have available the relevant information in a form that the individual can understand

➤ ensure they are aware of the potential risks to the individual and explain them clearly

➤ listen to the individual and observe for other responses.

The health record should include notes of a discussion about consent with the patient, including how understanding was checked and whether the patient continues to consent over time (NICE, 2006).

Summary

Consent means giving permission for something. Sometimes permission is withheld but there are things that care workers can do to establish consent where it is withheld. These actions are in keeping with an approach to care that respects the individual, improves care and sits securely within the legal framework for practice.

References

Collins Concise English Dictionary (2008), 'Consent', 7th edition, Glasgow, HarperCollins

Coulter, A. and Collins, A. (2011), *Making shared Decision-Making a Reality: No decision about me, without me*, London, King's Fund

NICE (2006), *Audit Criteria: Dementia: Supporting people with dementia and their carers in health and social care*, Clinical Guideline 42, London, National Institute for Health and Clinical Excellence

Continence

As many individuals who use health and social care services are elderly, infirm or have a disabling condition, continence is a significant issue. It is important to add that age, illness and impairment do not automatically lead to problems with continence, but a large number of individuals may seek advice or support for incontinence.

What are continence and incontinence?

Continence is normally described as the ability to maintain control over one's bladder and bowel functions. This will occur if the muscles and nerves located around the bladder, rectum and anal canal are in good working order. When an individual has specific problems with the bladder, it can result in urinary symptoms such as an overactive bladder and urge incontinence (Wilkinson, 2009). For the bowel, ignoring or delaying the need to go to the toilet may cause constipation. Prolonged constipation can eventually lead to haemorrhoids (dilated rectal veins) and confusion, especially in older people. When a person is doubly incontinent he or she has problems controlling both bladder and bowel functions.

A number of factors need to be considered in order to maintain continence (that is, having a fully functioning bladder and bowel), including:

➤ a healthy lifestyle with exercise

➤ a well-balanced diet free from fatty and spicy foods

➤ not smoking

➤ sensible alcohol intake

➤ at least eight glasses of water a day.

It is important for the individual to empty the bladder when the need arises and avoid stopping in midstream, as a delay could cause harm to the muscles controlling the bladder. A regular routine of exercise helps the digestive system to function normally and prevents the pelvic floor muscles from weakening. These muscles are necessary for the normal passing of urine and faeces and, if weak, can result in involuntary loss of urine and stool.

The care worker can encourage individuals to seek help and support if he or she notices any problems with their bladder or bowels. Individuals should be treated with respect, sensitivity and understanding. An assessment is normally the first step, as it will help to identify any underlying causes. NICE (2006) recommends a three-day bladder diary as a useful tool in assessing continence issues. For the bowels, it has been suggested that constipation management may be required unless there are more specific problems. NICE (2007) has published guidelines, easily accessible online, regarding bowel control problems.

Summary

Continence is normally described as the ability to maintain control over one's bladder and bowel function. A number of factors can lead to incontinence. There are ways in which care workers can support individuals to avoid problems with continence or manage incontinence.

References

NICE (2006), *Urinary Incontinence: The management of urinary incontinence in women*, Clinical Guideline 40, London, National Institute for Health and Clinical Excellence

NICE (2007), *Faecal Incontinence (Bowel Control Problems)*, London, National Institute for Health and Clinical Excellence

Wilkinson, K. (2009), 'A guide to assessing bladder function and urinary incontinence in older people', *Nursing Times*, 105 (40) [Online]

Cultural capability

As the population of the UK becomes increasingly diverse, the needs of different communities and groups of individuals must be considered when delivering health care. Cultural capability is an approach that can help practitioners engage with and communicate more effectively with a range of communities in culturally acceptable ways.

The importance of cultural capability

Cultural capability is an umbrella term that encourages anti-discriminatory practice and the development of evidenced-based skills and knowledge so that practitioners can work in culturally acceptable ways, thus becoming culturally competent (Papadopoulos, 2006). These skills embrace:

➤ cultural awareness – being aware of the similarities and differences between individuals' needs based on their ethnic, racial or religious backgrounds

➤ cultural sensitivity – being sensitive to the diverse ways that culture is demonstrated and celebrated

➤ cultural knowledge – knowing about a range of diverse needs and how they can be met.

The acquisition of these skills and knowledge can enable care workers to become culturally competent. To develop cultural competence, practitioners need to be self-aware and to recognise and challenge discriminatory and oppressive practice, such as racism.

Cultural capability requires practitioners to consider the ways in which they can develop the skills and knowledge to engage effectively with individuals, their families and their communities. It includes:

➤ becoming aware of one's biases and prejudices towards other cultures as well as one's own culture, and examining the differences between the cultures and their identities

➤ identifying deficits in cultural knowledge, especially individuals' beliefs, practices and lifestyles, and to overcome these deficits through study, reading or referring to interpreters

➤ avoiding stereotypical remarks and stigmatising assumptions

➤ avoiding making judgements about the individual when carrying out an assessment

➤ reflecting on how one respects, understands and responds to different ethnic histories, traditions, beliefs and value systems.

Summary

Cultural capability is an umbrella term that encourages anti-discriminatory practice and the development of evidenced-based skills and knowledge so that practitioners can work in culturally acceptable ways.

Cultural capability recognises diversity and encourages anti-discriminatory practice in the health and social care setting.

In order to become culturally competent, care workers need to develop specific skills and knowledge which can be applied to diverse groups.

References

Papadopoulos, I. (2006), *Transcultural Health and Social Care: Development of culturally competent practitioners*, London, Elsevier

Depersonalisation

Sometimes the quality of care that individuals receive is unacceptable. While care workers often have a very difficult job, there is no excuse for some practices that undermine the individuality of people in their care. One way a person's individuality is undermined is through depersonalisation.

What is depersonalisation?

Depersonalisation is a psychiatric condition related to anxiety. It is defined as an alteration in the perception or experience of the self so that one feels detached from one's mental processes or body (APA, 1994). It is about feeling as if you are not there, and not feeling any emotion.

When used in the context of health and social care, depersonalisation refers to the way that individuals feel after being subjected to poor quality care in which they are treated as if they were not a person but a task to be carried out. Depersonalisation is therefore the very opposite of person-centredness. The individual person is not at the centre of care, but subject to a routine or regime that sees him or her as an object for tasks to be done to instead of a person to work with.

Feelings of depersonalisation are a normal response to an overwhelming threat, according to Medford *et al* (2005). The threat might come from poor staff inflicting unacceptable care practices on vulnerable and often frail older people.

Unacceptable care is mostly likely to occur in an institutional setting such as a residential home for people with learning disabilities or for older people. Individuals in care can be depersonalised by:

➤ becoming dependent on others who know nothing about them

➤ being looked after by staff who pay no attention to what the person can do

➤ being treated as a helpless non-person

➤ being subject to rigid routines

➤ having personal preferences ignored.

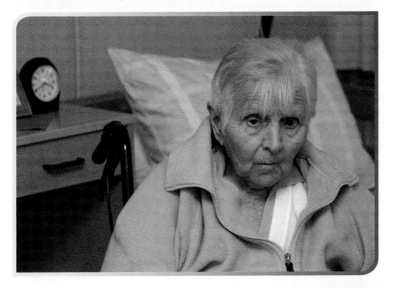

Summary

Depersonalisation is a psychiatric condition related to anxiety in which the person feels that they are not there. It can be caused by overwhelming threats such as poor care practices in homes for people with learning disabilities and older frail people.

References

APA (1994), *Diagnostic and Statistical Manual of Mental Disorders*, (DSM-IV), 4th edition, Washington DC, American Psychiatric Association

Medford, N., Sierra, M., Baker, D. and David, A.S. (2005), 'Understanding and treating depersonalisation disorder', *Advances in Psychiatric Treatment*, 11, 92–100

Deprivation of liberty

Individuals who enter health and social care may do so against their will. The Mental Health Act (2007) provides certain protection against misuse of powers, and the Mental Capacity Act (2005) provides a legal framework for making decisions on behalf of people who lack the capacity to make those decisions for themselves. These can be small decisions about which clothes to wear, or major decisions, such as about where to live or what treatment to have.

What is deprivation of liberty?

Where care might involve making decisions on behalf of vulnerable people, and therefore in a sense depriving them of (taking away) their liberty in either a hospital or a care home, legal safeguards have been introduced to protect their rights and ensure that the care they receive is in their best interests (MoJ, 2008). There is no legal definition of deprivation of liberty but the Alzheimer's Society (2010) lists examples that have been tested in courts of law, including:

➤ a patient being restrained in order to be admitted to hospital

➤ medication being given against a person's will

➤ staff having complete control over a patient's care or movements for a long period

➤ staff taking all decisions about a patient, including choices about assessments, treatment and visitors

➤ staff deciding whether a patient can be released into the care of others or to live elsewhere

➤ staff restricting a person's access to friends or family.

Three safeguards have been put in place to protect an individual's liberty. They are:

1. Provide the person whose liberty is at risk with a representative.

2. Allow the person to challenge any deprivation of liberty through the Court of Protection.

3. Provide a means of regularly reviewing and monitoring the deprivation of liberty (MoJ, 2008).

Summary

The Mental Capacity Act provides a legal framework for acting and making decisions on behalf of people who lack the capacity to make those decisions for themselves. Where this care might involve depriving vulnerable people of their liberty, legal safeguards have been introduced to protect their rights and ensure that the care they receive is in their best interests. The safeguards include being represented, allowing a legal challenge, and providing a means of reviewing and monitoring any deprivation.

References

Alzheimer's Society (2010), *Deprivation of Liberty Safeguards (DoLS)*, Factsheet 483, London, Alzheimer's Society

Mental Capacity Act 2005 (c. 9), London, The Stationery Office

Mental Health Act 2007 (c. 12), London, The Stationery Office

MoJ (2008), *Deprivation of Liberty Safeguards: Code of Practice to supplement the main Mental Capacity Act 2005 Code of Practice*, Ministry of Justice, London, The Stationery Office

Dignity

Better reporting of abuses of care in the early 21st century has led to concerns about individuals being treated poorly. One of the chief complaints has been about dignity being diminished. Quality care standards now demand that individuals are treated with dignity at every stage of their health and social care journey.

Promoting dignity

Dignity is about how people think, feel and behave in relation to the worth or value of themselves and others. To treat people with dignity is to treat them as being of worth, in a way that respects them as valued individuals. When dignity is absent from care, people feel devalued, and lacking in control and comfort. They may also lack confidence, be unable to make decisions for themselves, and feel humiliated, embarrassed and ashamed (RCN, 2008).

The way care is funded is a key determinant of dignity, especially in older age (JRF, 2004). Safeguarding dignity is also, however, about the care individuals receive that has been funded. Dignity has been linked to social inclusion, choice and independence. Dignified care requires workers to treat individuals with respect, compassion and sensitivity. When any or all of these aspects of care are missing, there is the potential for diminishing the dignity of individuals.

Care workers can help promote dignity in care by:

➤ providing care that takes account of cultural and other diversity, the need for privacy and sharing decision-making

➤ offering emotional support and being sensitive to the needs and comfort of others.

In practice this means individuals should be dressed appropriately for their age and gender, and if hospital gowns are used they should be fastened to avoid accidental exposure. Privacy should be provided for private conversations, intimate care, and personal activities such as going to the toilet.

The physical environment can also affect dignity. Bathroom and toilet facilities should be well maintained and cleaned regularly; curtains between beds should close properly to offer privacy; toilet doors should be closed when in use; and bays in wards should be single-sex (RCN, 2008).

A low level of personal allowance takes away individuals' personal dignity. This allowance should be able to pay expenses for clothes, personal items such as toiletries, spending on family and other costs apart from board, lodging and care services provided in care homes (Hirsch, 2006).

Summary

Dignity is about how people think, feel and behave in relation to the worth or value of themselves and others. Dignity means individuals being treated with respect, compassion and sensitivity.

References

Hirsch, D. (2006), *Five Costed Reforms to Long-Term Care Funding*, York, Joseph Rowntree Foundation

JRF (2004), *Funding Long-Term Care for Older People*, York, Joseph Rowntree Foundation

RCN (2008), 'Dignity: The RCN's definition of dignity', Royal College of Nursing, http://www.rcn.org.uk/__data/assets/pdf_file/0003/191730/003298.pdf (accessed 31 January 2013)

Discrimination

When people make assumptions about others, the care they give may not be appropriate. Likewise when people hold prejudices against others, the support they offer may not be what is necessary to meet the individual's needs. Broad generalisations about people, such as assumptions and prejudices, can lead to discrimination.

What is discrimination?

Discrimination is the prejudicial (harmful) treatment of an individual or group of individuals based on a trait or characteristic they possess. It is explicitly forbidden in UK law under the Disability and the Equality Act (2010), which sets out disabled people's rights in everyday life and protects individuals from disability discrimination.

These include the right to:

➤ access everyday goods and services

➤ buy and rent property

➤ join a club

➤ access functions of a public body.

Two examples of discrimination illustrate the ways in which certain groups are discriminated against. Older people can be denied health and social care services that anyone else would expect, because of their age. For instance, the Research on Age Discrimination Project (Bytheway et al, 2007) found that women over 70 were denied routine breast screening, even when they remain at risk of developing breast cancer. They were in effect denied access to the functions of a public body.

A second example is the situation of an individual with learning disabilities who is denied access to a sports club on the grounds that he would not 'fit in'. Reasonable efforts should be made by the club to support him in fitting in, to conform to the requirements of the Disability and Equality Act (2010) that everyone should be able to access everyday goods and services and join clubs.

Summary

Discrimination is the prejudicial treatment of an individual or group of individuals based on a personal characteristic. Some people who use health and social care services are more likely than others to be discriminated against. However, there is legislation against discriminatory practices.

References

Bytheway, B., Ward, R., Holland, C. and Peace, S. (2007), *Too Old: Older people's accounts of discrimination, exclusion and rejection. A report from the Research on Age Discrimination Project, (RoAD) to Help the Aged*, London, Help the Aged

HMG (2010), 'Disability and the Equality Act', Directgov, http://www.direct.gov.uk/en/DisabledPeople/RightsAndObligations/DG_4019061/ (accessed 30 August 2012)

Diversity

Diversity is fundamental to effective health and social care practice. The concept of diversity can mean different things to every individual. In an increasingly multicultural society with many black and minority ethnic communities, enabling diversity requires certain behaviours from everyone. These include respect, acceptance and understanding for all individuals. The rich uniqueness of individuals should be celebrated rather than being ignored or challenged, as everyone has the right to be treated with respect.

What is diversity?

Diversity is not easy to define; a dictionary definition describes it as the state or quality of being different or varied (*Collins Concise English Dictionary*, 2008). Another definition calls it 'the valuing of our individual differences and talents, creating a culture where everyone can participate, thrive and contribute' (NHS Information Centre, 2012). It is therefore not just about race and religion, but about a range of qualities. Diversity involves a positive attitude to difference or the variety of human characteristics. It claims to be about valuing difference and developing knowledge and understanding of different people and their beliefs and values.

➤ The differences between people should not be ignored.

➤ A shared understanding of difference should be promoted.

➤ Diversity means exploring the concept of difference in a safe and nurturing environment.

➤ It is necessary to developing skills and behaviours to provide effective care even when there is difference.

➤ It involves acting to overcome cultural barriers.

Summary

Diversity emphasises ideas about difference. It also involves a positive attitude to difference or the variety of human characteristics. It is about valuing difference and developing knowledge and understanding of different people and their beliefs and values.

References

Collins Concise English Dictionary (2008), 'Diversity', 7th edition, Glasgow, HarperCollins

NHS Information Centre (2012), 'Equality and diversity', NHS, http://www. ic.nhs.uk/equalityanddiversity/ (accessed 31 January 2013)

Duty of care

It is commonly understood that users of health and social care services should be offered care to meet their needs. In effect, professionals who work in care settings have a responsibility to uphold the interests of the individuals they look after. This is a duty of care.

What does the duty of care mean?

'Duty of care' is a term that has special significance in health and social care because the first obligation of care workers is to look after the people they are caring for. However, 'duty of care' is also a legal term: adults are obliged to be aware of the wellbeing of others and to take reasonable steps to avoid harming them through their actions or what they fail to do. Harm that can be reasonably foreseen includes physical, mental or economic harm.

The idea that an individual may be owed a duty of care by another person, even if they do not know each other, was established in law in the case of Donaghue v. Stevenson in 1932. In that case, after consuming ginger beer a customer had stomach problems. The legal ruling was that the manufacturer had a duty of care towards the consumer of the ginger beer, even though they had never met or had any prior relationship or interaction. Stevenson, the ginger beer manufacturer, was found to have been negligent for not taking sufficient care to ensure the product was free from a defect that was likely to cause injury or death (UK Law Online, 1998).

In many instances, users of care services are unable to take care of their own needs or may be vulnerable in other ways: children and older people, for instance. Care workers should therefore:

➤ put the needs and interests of people in their care first

➤ ensure that their actions and omissions do not cause harm to the people in their care.

There are steps care workers can take to uphold their duty of care to individuals:

1. Assess and intervene to meet physical, psychological and emotional needs.

2. Uphold and value the rights of service users as individuals.

3. Be aware of the potential for, and anticipate, risks to the individual and others.

4. Be aware of the potential for, and act against, exploitation, abuse and neglect.

Summary

Care workers must look after the people they are caring for and take reasonable steps to avoid physical, mental or economic harm. Care workers have a particular duty of care as clients can be vulnerable. There are steps they can take to uphold their duty of care.

References

UK Law Report (1998), *Donoghue (or McAlister) v. Stevenson*, [1932] All ER Rep 1, [1932] AC 562, House of Lords

Empowerment

Certain individuals or groups feel marginalised, with little control over aspects of their own lives. They might be excluded from deciding where they live or what food they eat. A key element of person-centred care is that individuals gain more control and are included in decisions that affect them. An approach that enables this is empowerment. While the term is widely used in business, philosophy, psychology, health and gender relations, here it is employed as a sociological term.

What is sociological empowerment?

Sociological empowerment is about individuals gaining control over aspects of their own lives, being involved in making decisions, and overcoming barriers to participation in everyday activities. It is closely linked to anti-discriminatory practice, and can have particular benefits to individuals with impairment or disability. It can also benefit other groups who might feel that they are unable to exert sufficient influence over their own lives, such as women in abusive relationships, or individuals subject to discriminations based on religion, ethnicity or race.

Disabled World (2010) offers an empowering model of disability that allows for the individual with a disability to take control of his or her treatment and access to services. A professional who works with that individual becomes a service provider who offers guidance and follows the individual's wishes. The model therefore empowers the individual to pursue his or her own goals.

Every worker in health and social care can help empower

individuals, as a service provider, by supporting the individuals in his or her care:

➤ to make decisions that affect their lives

➤ to gain access to information and resources to help them make informed decisions

➤ in choosing between different options

➤ by being positive about their abilities

➤ by improving their skills

➤ by promoting a positive perception through education and engagement.

Summary

Empowerment is about individuals gaining control over aspects of their own lives, being involved in making decisions, and overcoming barriers to participation in everyday activities. Professionals who work with that individual become service providers offering guidance and following the individual's wishes in areas such as decision-making, skills development and positive perceptions.

References

Disabled World (2010), 'Glossary list of definitions and explanations of the models of disability in society today', http://www.disabled-world.com/definitions/disability-models.php (accessed 31 January 2013)

Equality

In the UK there are legal requirements to promote equality in connection with disability, gender and race. Equality is generally associated with promoting the right to be different. Under the Equality Act (2010) the focus has been on eliminating discrimination and reducing inequalities in the workplace and in wider society. The Act sets out different ways in which it is unlawful to discriminate against an individual or groups of individuals whether directly or indirectly, or through harassment or victimisation.

What is equality?

The Equality Act (2010) defines equality as ensuring individuals or groups of individuals are treated fairly and equally and no less favourably than is specific to their needs. Individuals should be given choice, be valued and have a right to determine the course of their own lives. Many professional health and social care organisations, such as the Nursing and Midwifery Council (NMC, 2008), which regulates nursing and midwifery practice, require that their members do not discriminate against any individual or groups of individuals.

The Equality Act offers protection in relation to the following nine characteristics:

➤ **Age**: a person may belong to an age group such as the elderly

➤ **Disability**: either a physical or mental impairment

➤ **Gender reassignment**: a person has the protected characteristic of gender reassignment if the person is proposing to undergo, is undergoing or has undergone a process (or part of a process) for the purpose of reassigning the person's sex by changing physiological or other attributes of sex

➤ **Marriage or civil partnership**: a person has the protected characteristic of marriage and civil partnership if the person is married or is a civil partner

➤ **Race**: including colour, nationality and ethnic or national origins; the fact that a racial group comprises two or more distinct groups does not prevent it from constituting a particular racial group

➤ **Religion or belief**: including any religion or lack of religion; belief means any religious or philosophical belief or lack of belief

➤ **Sex**: both male and female

➤ **Sexual orientation**: whether towards persons of the same sex, persons of the opposite sex, or persons of either sex

➤ **Pregnancy and maternity**: being pregnant or having given birth.

Summary

Equality is about ensuring individuals or groups of individuals are treated fairly and equally and no less favourably than is specific to their needs. It stresses fairness and promotes the right to be different. The Equality Act (2010) has helped to ensure that individuals are not discriminated against, harassed or victimised regardless of their personal characteristics, beliefs or values.

References

Equality Act 2010 (c. 15), London, The Stationery Office

NMC (2008), *The Code: Standards of conduct, performance and ethics for nurses and midwives*, London, Nursing and Midwifery Council

Ethics

Living in a complex society requires moral standards that determine how we behave towards one another. For example, cheating and lying are generally frowned upon. In health and social care, ideas about ethics play a significant part in the way people interact.

What are ethical principals?

Ethics provide moral principles that guide the care that is delivered. Decisions workers make are based on their values and their judgement in each situation they encounter. They are, however, given guidance in these values and judgements.

Ethics are important because they are moral guides for the way people lead their lives, including when they are at work. They encompass

➤ rights and responsibilities

➤ what is good and what is bad.

It is evident how they might apply to health and social care, and why professional regulatory bodies, such as the Nursing and Midwifery Council, are keen to include ethical principles in their codes of conduct. In fact, the full title of the code of conduct includes the words 'Standards of conduct, performance and ethics' (NMC, 2008).

One of the best-known frameworks for ethical care is that of Beauchamp and Childress (2001) in which they set out four basic principles as follows:

➤ **Respect for autonomy**: Individuals have a right to take part in decisions about their own care and treatment.

➤ **Beneficence**: Practitioners have a duty to act in the best interests of the individual.

➤ **Non-maleficence**: Practitioners should not harm individuals.

➤ **Justice**: Practitioners should act fairly and treat individuals equally.

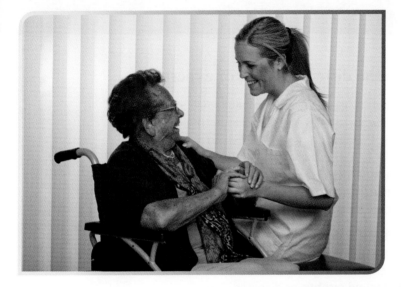

Summary

Ethics are moral guides for the way people lead their lives and have special relevance to care work. They include respect for individual autonomy, the duty to do good and not to harm the individual, and to act fairly.

References

Beauchamp, T.L. and Childress, J.F. (2001), *Principles of Medical Ethics*, Oxford, Oxford University Press

NMC (2008), *The Code: Standards of conduct, performance and ethics for nurses and midwives*, London, Nursing and Midwifery Council

Experts

People in care value services that are offered in partnership with them, and that are user focused (Innes *et al*, 2006). Quality is therefore measured partly by the extent to which individuals are supported in shaping the services they receive. Two terms have been coined that acknowledge and illustrate partnership working between care providers and individuals who use health and social care services: 'expert by experience', and 'the expert patient'.

What are the different types of expert?

The term 'expert by experience' describes someone who has used social care services, and refers to his or her direct involvement in the development, delivery and evaluation of services (CSCI, 2007). The idea behind the term is that people who use services are in a better position through their experience to know what services are needed and how they should be provided.

The Expert Patient Programme is a self-management programme for people who are living with a chronic (long-term) condition such as rheumatoid arthritis or diabetes. The aim is to support individuals with long-term conditions by increasing their confidence, improving their quality of life, and helping them manage their condition more effectively (NHS Choices, 2010). The term acknowledges that the person understands how the condition affects him or her, and armed with this knowledge is an expert in the experience of being a patient with a long-term condition.

Summary

Care users value services that are offered in partnership with them, and that are user focused. Two terms, 'expert by experience' and 'the expert patient', have been coined that acknowledge and illustrate partnership working between care providers and individuals who use health and social care services.

References

CSCI (2007), *People Who Use Services and Experts by Experience*, London, Commission for Social Care Inspection

Innes, A., Macpherson, S. and McCabe, L. (2006), *Promoting Person-Centred Care at the Frontline*, York, Joseph Rowntree Foundation/SCIE

NHS Choices (2010), 'The Expert Patients Programme (EPP)', http://www.nhs.uk/conditions/Expert-patients-programme-/Pages/Introduction.aspx/ (accessed 31 January 2013)

FACS

One of the consequences of providing a greater proportion of health and social care in community settings instead of in institutions, such as hospitals and residential care homes, is that the demand on resources has outgrown the capacity to provide services. Resources therefore need to be better targeted at individuals who need them most. One way of doing this is by a system that prioritises care, giving access to care to those who need it most.

What is Fair Access to Care Services (FACS)?

The Department of Health (2010) issued a document that aimed to prioritise need in the context of putting people first in adult social care in England. It provided guidance on eligibility criteria, which is underpinned by assessment of individual need. Based on the assessment, individuals would be placed within one of four bands:

➤ low needs, for example where the individual is unable to carry out one or two personal care or domestic routines

➤ moderate needs, for example where the individual is unable to perform several personal care or domestic routines

➤ substantial needs, for example where the individual has or will have only partial choice and control over the immediate environment, or there is risk of abuse or neglect

➤ critical needs, for example where there is a threat to life or there is a serious health problem.

Local authorities may provide community services to adults with needs arising from physical, sensory, learning or cognitive disabilities or mental health problems.

Summary

Offering community care services to adults depends on the availability of resources. To prioritise care for those in greatest need, the Fair Access to Care Services framework aims to put people first and target care where it is most needed.

References

DH (2010), *Prioritising Need in the Context of 'Putting People First': A whole system approach to eligibility for social care. Guidance on eligibility criteria for adult social care, England 2010*, Best Practice Guidance, London, Department of Health

Family support

All families need help and support when faced with a crisis, regardless of their income, education or lifestyle. This support may vary depending on the situation, but often in times of distress practical, psychological, social and/or emotional help may be needed. Those who support families tend to be family members and close friends, but there are occasions when more formal systems of support are required.

What is family support?

Family support is quite a difficult term to define but Dolan *et al* (2006) describe it as both a style of work and a set of activities that reinforce positive informal social networks. The primary focus is on early intervention, which promotes and protects the health and wellbeing of children, young people and their families, including those who are vulnerable and at risk. Other definitions emphasise helping families to build a strong foundation that fosters growth and development.

The Troubled Families Programme resulted from the summer riots of 2011 amid concerns about parenting and family life. The research report *Family Action* identifies the need for a system-wide approach that recommends:

➤ a whole-family approach, working with parents and children

➤ coordination of multiagency support using a key-worker model

➤ tailoring packages of support

➤ an assessment process for family strengths and weaknesses

➤ a clearly understood model that provides a structure for prioritising and evaluating actions (Family Action, 2012).

The Family Star model advocated in *Family Action* evaluates needs and outcomes based on an eight-point structure:

1. meeting emotional needs

2. promoting good health

3. providing home and money

4. keeping a family routine

5. keeping your child safe

6. setting boundaries

7. supporting learning

8. a supportive social life.

Summary

Family support is described as a style of work and a set of activities that reinforce positive informal social networks. When faced with a difficult situation or a crisis, families cope with support from family members and close friends. However, there are certain occasions when families seek help from more formal networks and agencies that will support them during these critical times. A system-wide approach and adoption of the Family Star model can support families to overcome difficulties.

References

Dolan, P., Canavan, J. and Pinkerton, J. (2006), *Family Support as Reflective Practice*, London, Jessica Kingsley

Family Action (2012), *Family Action: The Troubled Families Programme*, http://www.family-action.org.uk/uploads/documents/The%20 Troubled%20Families%20Programme-What's%20needed%20to%20 deliver%20outcomes%20on%20school%20attendance%20FINAL.pdf (accessed 31 January 2013)

Fertility

Fertility is an important issue for both women and men as they look forward to pregnancy and the birth of a baby. For many couples this may take place within a year if they do not use contraception and have regular sexual intercourse.

Fertility and infertility

Female fertility is the ability to conceive a child after having regular sex without any contraceptives. It is important that women understand their menstrual cycle. The egg survives for only a day or two so there is limited time each month – about six days – in which the woman can get pregnant.

Some women and men have trouble conceiving. Some of the causes of female infertility include the following:

➤ Polycystic ovary syndrome (PCOS) – this involves infrequent menstrual periods and lack of regular ovulation. Women with PCOS meet at least two out of three of the following criteria: polycystic ovaries, the failure or cessation of ovulation, and excessive production of male sex hormones. Other conditions frequently associated with PCOS are obesity, hypertension, type 2 diabetes and cardiovascular risk (Royal College of Obstetricians and Gynaecologists, 2012a).

➤ Premature ovarian failure – ovaries fail to function and menstruation stops before age 40.

➤ Fibroids – benign tumours of the uterus which may cause painful periods, and abdominal, pelvic or lower-back discomfort (Royal College of Obstetricians and Gynaecologists, 2012b).

➤ Uterine factors – there are a variety of factors related to the function of the uterus which prevent an embryo from implanting and developing.

➤ Endometriosis – tissue from the lining of the uterus migrates outside the uterus and causes painful, heavy periods, lower-back and pelvic pain (American College of Obstetricians and Gynecologists, 2012).

Common causes of infertility in men include pre-testicular problems, obesity, and sperm problems, such as low sperm count and low sperm motility.

Of the couples who do not conceive in the first year, about half will do so in the second year (NICE, 2004). Female fertility declines with age, but the effect on fertility in men is not as clear. If concerned about their fertility or to optimise the chance of a pregnancy, the couple should engage in sexual intercourse every two to three days.

Women who are trying to become pregnant should not drink any more than one or two units of alcohol once or twice a week, and avoid becoming intoxicated. Men should also avoid excessive alcohol intake as it is detrimental to semen quality. Smoking is likely to reduce women's fertility and men's semen quality, so both sexes should avoid smoking. It should be noted that women and men who have a body mass index of more than 29 are likely to take longer to conceive.

Summary

Many couples who are fertile will conceive a baby within a year without problems. However, where fertility is an issue and the woman fails to conceive, fertility treatments are available. The key to having a healthy baby is to engage in a healthy lifestyle when planning a pregnancy.

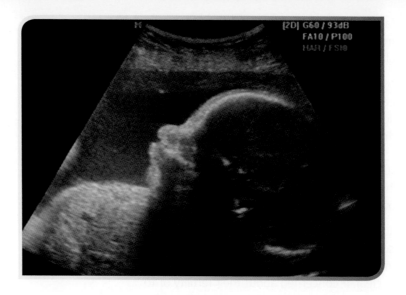

References

American College of Obstetricians and Gynecologists (2012), 'FAQ 137: Treating infertility', http://www.acog.org/~/media/ For%20Patients/faq013.pdf?dmc=1&ts=20121221T0659480003 (accessed 30 January 2013)

NICE (2004), *Fertility: Assessment and treatment for people with fertility problems*, Clinical Guideline 11, National Institute for Health and Clinical Excellence, http://www.nice.org.uk/nicemedia/pdf/CG011niceguideline.pdf (accessed 31 January 2013)

Royal College of Obstetricians and Gynaecologists (2012a), 'RCOG release: Doctors advise on treatment for the long-term consequences of polycystic ovary syndrome', http://www.rcog.org.uk/news/rcog-release-doctors-advise-treatment-long-term-consequences-polycystic-ovary-syndrome/ (accessed 31 January 2013)

Royal College of Obstetricians and Gynaecologists (2012b), *Clinical Recommendations on the Use of Uterine Artery Embolisation in the Management of Fibroids*, http://www.rcog.org.uk/files/rcog-corp/ uploaded-files/WPRUterineArteryEmbolisation2009.pdf/ (accessed 31 January 2013)

Health

There is a saying that if you haven't got your health, you haven't got anything. It is debatable whether this is really true, but it does sum up the importance people attribute to health, and by implication the consequences of not being healthy. But what is health?

What does being healthy mean?

Health or wellness is often viewed as a continuum (a continuous sequence) based on the work of Travis (1975). On the continuum are the polar events of a premature death at one end, and at the other end a state of high levels of wellness. Being reasonably fit and with no obvious signs of illness would place a person in the middle of the continuum, in a neutral zone.

This way of picturing health is far from the definition given by the World Health Organization (WHO, 1946/2006), in which health is 'a state of complete physical, mental and social wellbeing, and not merely the absence of disease or infirmity'. This definition sounds more like an aspiration than something that can be achieved – when even the healthiest people on Travis's continuum might find it difficult to achieve complete bodily, psychological and relational fulfilment. It also implies a fixed state of being healthy, whereas a continuum suggests people can move back and forwards as their health fluctuates.

The concept of the health field (Lalonde, 1981) complemented Travis's ideas. The health field envisaged health as four interdependent categories that determined the level of a person's health:

➤ lifestyle and personal decisions
➤ environmental factors over which individuals do not have control
➤ genetic and biomedical make-up
➤ health-care organisation.

Simple models and definitions cannot convey complex ideas. What is certain, however, is that health, whatever definition or model individuals adhere to, continues to be the focus of public policy and individual concern.

Summary

Different models and definitions of health convey a complex mix of ideas, from health being a continuum to categorisation as interdependent fields. Health seems to embody different elements, some that individuals can control and others that they have limited or no control over.

References

Lalonde, M. (1981), *A New Perspective on the Health of Canadians*, Ottawa, Ministry of Supply and Services, Government of Canada

Travis, J.W. (1975), 'Illness–Wellness continuum' in 'A new vision of wellness', Well People, http://www.wellpeople.com/What_Is_Wellness.aspx (accessed 5 October 2012)

WHO (1946/2006), *Constitution of the World Health Organization*, Basic Documents, 45th edition, Supplement, Geneva, World Health Organization

Health promotion

A major policy driver since the last decade of the 20th century has been to complement disease prevention with actions to promote health. This is most noticeable, perhaps, in phrases such as 'a healthy lifestyle' which accompany arguments about obesity, diabetes and the benefits of exercise and not smoking.

What is health promotion?

Health promotion is about raising the health status of individuals and communities (Ewles and Simnett, 2005). It is essential in addressing the major health challenges, including communicable and non-communicable diseases and issues related to human development and health.

Health promotion is a process. It enables people to take action:

➤ It is not something that is done on or to people; it is done by, with and for people either as individuals or as groups.

➤ It strengthens the skills and capabilities of individuals to take action and the capacity of groups or communities to act collectively.

➤ It helps individuals and groups to exert control over the determinants of health and achieve positive change (Public Health Agency, 2009).

Ewles and Simnett (2005) outline a framework of five approaches to health promotion:

1. the medical approach, which seeks to intervene to minimise the rate of disease and disability

2. the behaviour change approach, which aims to change people's attitudes and behaviour so that they adopt a healthy lifestyle

3. the educational approach, in which well-informed decisions are made based on knowledge and understanding of health issues

4. the client-centred approach, which helps individuals to identify their own health needs and to make their own decisions and choices

5. the societal change approach, which effects change on the physical, social and economic environment in order to make it more conducive (favourable) to good health.

Effective health promotion strategies tend to use a blend of each of these approaches, even if some are more prominent than others.

Summary

Health promotion is about raising the health status of individuals and communities. There are various approaches to health promotion: medical, behavioural, educational, client-centred and societal, but effective strategies tend to use a blend of different approaches.

References

Ewles, L. and Simnett, I. (2005), *Promoting Health: A practical guide*, 3rd edition, London, Scutari Press

Public Health Agency (2009), 'What is health promotion?', http://www.healthpromotionagency.org.uk/Healthpromotion/Health/section2.htm/ (accessed 8 October 2012)

Healthy neighbourhoods

One of the factors that influence people's health is where they live. The Acheson Report (1998) outlined the connection between poor health and living in a deprived area. The report showed that every aspect of health is worse for people living in deprived circumstances. In turn this gave rise to the idea of healthy neighbourhoods.

What are healthy neighbourhoods?

Acheson distinguished between people's personal characteristics, such as their age and gender, and their surroundings. Policy could not change people's age or gender but it could impact on their environment.

The idea of healthy neighbourhoods was introduced shortly thereafter with a government paper, *Saving Lives: Our healthier nation* (Department of Health, 1999). This paper proposed that public health interventions be aimed at healthy schools, healthy workplaces and healthy neighbourhoods.

In practice a healthy neighbourhood is a place where:

➤ people feel safe and included

➤ the environment is clean and unpolluted

➤ people can express their health needs

➤ new ideas are encouraged.

Community resources or the lack of them can have a significant impact on the wellbeing and health of the people who live there. Resources include amenities, local knowledge, accessible services, employment opportunities and funding to build healthy neighbourhoods.

Summary

People's health is influenced by where they live, and policy interventions are aimed at creating healthy schools, healthy workplaces and healthy neighbourhoods. Resources are required to build healthy neighbourhoods.

References

Acheson, D. (1998), *Independent Inquiry into Inequalities in Health*, (Acheson Report), London, The Stationery Office

Department of Health (1999), *Saving Lives: Our healthier nation*, Cm 4386, London, The Stationery Office

Holistic approach to care

There is always more to a person than you can see, and health and social care providers are encouraged to take into account more than first impressions. A person-centred approach to care requires that the whole person is taken into account, not just the individual's illness or disability. Looking at the whole person is called holism.

What is holism?

Holism is an approach to health that acknowledges health depends upon many interrelated components, which interact in such a way that the overall effect constitutes health or illness (Wade, 2009). These components are:

➤ psychological – the individual's self-esteem or self-worth

➤ spiritual – the meaning life has for the individual

➤ physical – biological health or disability

➤ environmental – the individual's living environment and economic status

➤ social – the individual's relationships.

In practice, holistic care begins with a biographical approach in which details of the person's life, values and relationships are gathered. This informs care based on the individual's strengths, aspirations and preferences; each decision is built on information based on the individual's psychological, spiritual, physical, environmental and social background.

Summary

Holism refers to an approach to health that recognises health depends upon many interrelated components, which interact in such a way that the overall effect constitutes health or illness. Psychological, spiritual, physical, environmental and social components each interact to constitute health or ill-health.

References

Wade, D. (2009), *Holistic Health Care: What is it, and how can we achieve it?*, Oxford, Oxford Centre for Enablement

Home

According to Davies (2000), most care of older people takes place in their own homes. With the acceleration of community care policies in the decade since Davies made this assertion, it is now safe to say that most care does take place in people's homes, whether it is care for older people, individuals with a learning disability, a child or young person, or someone who has mental health problems.

What is 'home'?

Home can be defined as the place where a person lives, or as a house or other dwelling (*Collins Concise English Dictionary*, 2008). However, home is not just about where a person lives or only the bricks and mortar, or whether they live with a family, other individuals or alone. Home has many alternative meanings for individuals, and these meanings become more apparent when people leave or lose their home. It is important, therefore, to gain an understanding of the emotional attachment people feel for their home.

For different people, home might be one or a combination of the following:

➤ a physical environment where particular design and structural features are important; for example, the home might be a bungalow that has been adapted to cater for a wheelchair user

➤ a social environment in which the individual takes on a particular role, such as a father or a grandmother

➤ a psychological environment where the individual can feel in control of his or her life and therefore have a greater sense of self-confidence and personal esteem.

However, while these different environments can be enabling for people, it should be remembered that home can also be a disabling environment. A disabling home environment is one where an individual's ability to function in everyday ways is impaired. This might be because of:

➤ a physical environment that is unsuitable or has not been adapted as required; for example, it may have plug sockets that are too low for an older person to reach

➤ a social environment where the individual is not able to fulfil a role; he or she might be isolated and lonely

➤ a psychological environment where the person is being abused, for example through being denied visitors.

In our modern Western society, most people do not live their whole lives in one home. They move around: going to university, following a job, or marrying. In most circumstances they leave one home and go to another, often through choice. However, some people do not choose to leave their home: they lose their home.

Losing a home is a traumatic event that many older people endure when they can no longer be cared for in their own home. Losing a home has consequences that in some ways are similar to bereavement. Individuals might lose:

➤ many of their personal belongings

➤ their social role as a neighbour or husband/wife

➤ their independence

> their feelings of attachment to a place

> their choice of company and relationships.

Summary

Home has different meanings: it is a physical, social and psychological environment. Home can also be a disabling environment if it is unsuitable or not adapted to the needs of the individual; if the person is isolated or lonely; or if it is a place that contributes to psychological problems for the individual. Losing one's home, however, can result in losses similar in some ways to bereavement.

References

Collins Concise English Dictionary (2008), 7th edition, Glasgow, HarperCollins

Davies, M. (2000), *The Blackwell Encyclopaedia of Social Work*, Oxford, Blackwell

Identity

Much of the discussion about identity is concerned with personal identity. What makes a person unique, and what is the set of characteristics that makes that individual identifiable? Developing a sense of identity is an essential part of everyone's life, and most of the time people are fairly certain about their identity. However, this is not always the case. For example, individuals who have not lived with their birth parents may need to recover their past.

What is identity and why is it important?

A secure sense of identity is vital to health and development. Children who grow up in families that they are born into have the opportunity to find out about the members of their immediate and extended family, and about their background. Others who are separated at a young age may have gaps in their identity and may have to find out about painful memories or other emotions. As another example, individuals who have difficulty communicating things about themselves due to some form of disability often find assumptions are made about their identity.

Erikson (1968) developed a psychosocial theory of identity. He discovered that the community in which children and adolescents live helps to shape their identity. Erikson believed that identity was a lifelong developmental process involving a resolution of conflicts. He considered these conflicts to be common to most people and therefore typical.

Another important theory of identity is social construction. Phoenix (2002) believes identity is constructed through social relations including language, our interactions with other people, and the ways in which our society treats certain groups of people.

Individuals who lose their identities, for example through separation from parents at birth, need to reconstruct their identities. Life-story work has been used to help with this reconstruction. Individuals who work with children and young people have used this approach as it helps children to talk about their losses and separations and all the other things happening in their lives. By telling the story, identity is constructed in a particular way. Bruner (1990) suggests that we make ourselves and our identities through the stories about ourselves that we tell others and ourselves.

Identities can also be threatened by long-term conditions that disrupt a person's life. Illness may be stigmatising, and the individual may try to keep it hidden rather than making it known to others within the wider society. Life stories can help these individuals too to construct their identity in a particular way to put forward who they are.

Summary

Identity is an important component of an individual but it can develop and change in time. Two well-known theories, Erikson's psychosocial theory of identity and Phoenix's theory of social construction, have been put forward as explanations of how identity is shaped. Identity is not fixed or static but is always in the process of being formed. Life-story work can help individuals to reconstruct their identities when using a social construction approach.

References

Bruner, J. (1990), *Acts of Meaning*, Cambridge, Harvard University Press

Erikson, E. (1968), *Identity: Youth and crisis*, New York, W.W. Norton

Phoenix, A. (2002), 'Identities and diversities' in Miell, D., Phoenix, A. and Thomas, K. (eds), *Mapping Psychology*, vol. 1, Milton Keynes, Open University

Institutionalisation

Modern society is made up of institutions: the NHS, the justice system and the royal family are examples of three very different types of institution in the UK today. However, when people think about institutions they often recall old-fashioned images such as the workhouse or mental asylums. And being sent to one of these places conjures up the fear of institutionalisation.

What is institutionalisation?

Institutionalisation is the process of committing an individual or groups of people to an institution such as a hospital or a prison. Becoming institutionalised is what happens to an individual who has spent many years in a hospital, especially because of mental illness or learning disabilities. Even though most of the old asylum-type institutions are now closed, the concept of institutionalisation remains relevant to health and social care today. Individuals can still become institutionalised; for example, when they are admitted to a residential home for older people.

However, being institutionalised is not just about spending a long time in a hospital or residential home. Particular characteristics are attached to the idea. Goffman, a sociologist, studied long-stay mental hospitals and coined the term 'total institution' to reflect the way that being an inmate of the asylum takes over the individual's life completely.

Goffman (1961, p. 11) defines a total institution as 'a place of residence where a large number of like-situated individuals, cut off from wider society for an appreciable length of time, together lead an enclosed, formally administered round of life'. Jones and Fowles (2008) outline four main characteristics of a total institution:

➤ batch living, in which people are treated as if they are all the same with strict rules over their behaviour

➤ binary management, in which staff and inmates are separated by two different sets of rules

➤ an inmate role that strips individuals of their individuality and imposes an identity the institution chooses

➤ an institutional perspective where the individual's way of life is taken over by the needs of the institution.

Community care has resulted in old institutions that used to house large numbers of patients for years being closed, but it is vital that new forms of institution do not replicate the mistakes of the past and institutionalise service users in community settings.

Summary

Institutionalisation is the process of committing an individual or groups of people into an institution such as a hospital or a prison where they lose their individuality through batch living, binary management, and adopting the inmate role and the institution's perspective. There are risks that community care might lead to a new form of institutionalisation.

References

Goffman, E. (1961), *Asylums: Essays on the social situation of mental patients and other inmates*, Harmondsworth, Penguin

Jones, K. and Fowles, A.J. (2008), 'Total institutions' in Johnson, J. and De Souza, C. (eds), *Understanding Health and Social Care: An introductory reader*, 2nd edition, London and Los Angeles, Sage

Integrated living

A key priority for policy in the 21st century has been to promote independence among individuals who use health and social care services. However, being independent is not just about doing everything for yourself, as everyone in society is to some extent interdependent. We all rely on each other, even if for different reasons.

What is integrated and independent living?

Disabled people often need assistance in everyday life, but they can still live independently even when they cannot do everything for themselves. There is some variation in how integrated living is supported, with some individuals employing their own personal assistants and others using dedicated provision resourced by local authorities. As the Leicestershire Centre for Integrated Living (2010) states, it is a fundamental understanding of choice and control.

Disabled people can be included when they are in a position to have the same choice and control over their own lives as others. This means having access to finances and support to enable disabled people to employ their own assistants to support them with their everyday lives. Such support helps to facilitate independence. By employing their own staff, disabled people can control how the assistance they need is provided, allowing them to lead the lifestyle of their choice.

Typically, integrated living teams help people of working age with long-term severe or complex physical impairments. The Dudley Metropolitan Borough Council Disability

Support Team (formerly the Integrated Living Team), for example, offers to:

➤ address all aspects of an individual's life including health, wellbeing, self-esteem, independence, social and leisure activities

➤ provide improved care and health outcomes, individual choices and action plans for their clients

➤ build strong networks with employment and educational services (2012).

Summary

Disabled people often need assistance in everyday life, but they can still live independently even when they cannot do everything for themselves. It is a matter of choice and control. Integrated or independent living might be supported through personal assistants or by a team of support workers.

References

Dudley Metropolitan Borough Council (2012), 'Disability Support Team (formerly known as the Integrated Living Team)', http://www.dudley.gov.uk/resident/care-health/adult-health-social-care/how-to-contact-adult-social-care-services/integrated-living-team/ (accessed 31 January 2013)

Leicestershire Centre for Integrated Living (2010), 'Introduction to independent or integrated living', http://www.lcil.org.uk/About_Us/Independent_Living/ (accessed 31 January 2013)

Intimate care

Providing intimate care can be one of the most challenging duties that workers in health and social care carry out. It can be embarrassing for the care worker and it can be embarrassing for the recipient of care.

Providing intimate care

Intimacy refers to being deeply personal and private (*Collins Concise English Dictionary*, 2008). With intimate care, personal and social boundaries are crossed. This can make it difficult to evaluate what is acceptable behaviour and what is not acceptable behaviour.

Most people are unaccustomed to other people seeing and touching their bodies when using the toilet, showering, dressing, or being given assistance at mealtimes. Providing personal care breaks the usual social rules about behaviour when it involves attending to bodily functions that people are brought up to keep private. Yet this is an intrinsic part of many health and social care workers' roles, and it is an aspect of work that needs to be carried out while respecting and maintaining the dignity and privacy of service users (GSCC, 2010).

Providing intimate care also involves a cultural element. Lawler (1991) found that female nurses had more difficulty managing intimate care with male patients than male nurses did with female patients. And in some cultures it is not acceptable for female patients to receive any form of intimate care from men.

There are ways in which health and social care workers can deliver intimate care that overcome some of the social awkwardness of touching another person. Care workers should:

➤ be trained and prepared for the particular work they are expected to carry out

➤ have necessary equipment including protective gloves

➤ be aware of any cultural element to the personal care

➤ ask about the individual's personal preferences

➤ maintain eye contact or look the other way as appropriate, and try to disguise their own embarrassment

➤ use terminology familiar to the individual

➤ discuss what is to be done with the individual.

Summary

Intimate care crosses personal and social boundaries. It can be embarrassing for both the care provider and the care receiver, and yet it is a normal aspect of the role of health and social care workers. There are ways workers can provide intimate care that alleviate some of the social awkwardness and make it more acceptable.

References

Collins Concise English Dictionary (2008), 'Intimate', 7th edition, Glasgow, HarperCollins

GSCC (2010), 'Codes of Practice for Social Care Workers', London, General Social Care Council

Lawler, J. (1991), *Behind the Screens: Nursing, somology and the problem of the body*, Melbourne, Churchill Livingstone

KLORA

In health and social care there is an expectation that services are judged by what they do; that is, on the quality of the service they provide. The quality of their provision is measured by a range of outcomes. When judging the quality of care given in homes for adults and older people in England, the way the outcomes are measured is through the **key lines of regulatory assessment (KLORA)**.

Key lines of regulatory assessment

KLORA (key lines of regulatory assessment) were developed by the Commission for Social Care Inspection (CSCI, 2007) to judge how well a care-home provider delivers outcomes for the people who are users of the care home. This judgement is based on the standards examined during the inspection process, and the service is rated as either excellent, good, adequate or poor for each outcome group.

There are eight outcome groups, which are summarised as follows:

1. **Choice of home**: having information available to make an informed choice of home

2. **Individual needs and choices**: individuals playing an active role in choosing and planning their support

3. **Lifestyle and daily life**: individuals choosing and being supported in their lifestyle choice, including educational, cultural and recreational activities

4. **Personal health and care support**: individuals receiving respectful care that maintains dignity and privacy

5. **Concerns, complaints and protection**: individuals being able to voice concerns, have their rights protected and be protected from abuse

6. **Environment**: a physical layout for the facility that is safe, comfortable and maintained in a way that encourages independence

7. **Staffing**: having sufficient numbers of trained and skilled staff

8. **Conduct and management of the home**: openness and respect underpinning the management of the home, as well as effective quality assurance measures developed by a qualified, competent manager.

Summary

KLORA were developed by the Commission for Social Care Inspection to make a judgement on the quality of care homes for adults in England. The judgement is based on the standards in eight outcome groups looked at during an inspection. The care home is rated as either excellent, good, adequate or poor for each outcome group.

References

CSCI (2007), *Key Lines of Regulatory Assessment (KLORA): Care homes for adults (Younger adults 18–65 and older people)*, Quality, Performance and Methods Directorate, Commission for Social Care Inspection

Life-story work

Many people reflect on their past life and become nostalgic for people they have met and places they have visited. However, for many users of health and social care services there are gaps in their recollections; examples are older people with dementia and children who were separated from their parents and home at an early age. One way of helping individuals to recapture memories or foster a greater sense of identity is through life-story work.

What is life-story work?

Life-story work is a way of working with people to explore their life experiences in order to help them come to terms with difficulties or challenging life transitions. It can give back a sense of self to a person. It is a type of biographical approach and has been used with a variety of different individuals, including:

➤ children being prepared for fostering or adoption

➤ older people with dementia

➤ individuals with learning disabilities

➤ people in hospices.

Life-story work can take the form of a book, scrapbook, photo album or a collection of personal items.

Ryan and Walker (2007) say that life-story work can increase a child's sense of self-esteem, as children who are separated from their families often think that they are worthless and unloved. It is helpful in contributing to children's understanding of their past, their present and their future. It allows recording of significant information and events for children to refer to when they are older or as they grow up, such as a description of their birth family, where they were born, significant people in their lives, and their care history (Be My Parent, 2007).

Life-story work is a means to enhance the care provided to older people, particularly those with dementia. The benefits for individuals, families/friends and for staff providing care include:

➤ improving understanding of the individual

➤ promoting relationships

➤ facilitating delivery of person-centred care (Dementia UK, 2012).

Summary

Life-story work is a way of working with people to explore their life experiences in order to help them come to terms with difficulties or challenging life transitions. It can increase a child's sense of esteem and enhance the care provided to older people with dementia.

References

Be My Parent (2007), 'What is life story work and why is it important?', http://www.bemyparent.org.uk/info-for-families/your-questions/what-is-life-story-work-and-why-is-it-important,128,AR.html (accessed 31 January 2013)

Dementia UK (2012), 'Life story work', http://www.dementiauk.org/information-support/life-story-work/ (accessed 31 January 2013)

Ryan, T. and Walker, R. (2007), *Life Story Work: A practical guide to helping children understand their past*, revised edition, London, British Association for Adoption and Fostering

Mediation

Have you ever had an argument with someone with whom you cannot agree? Sometimes you might want to compromise, for example over where you go for a holiday with your partner. At other times it is useful to ask someone else to help you see things the way others see them. Being helped to compromise is a form of mediation.

Using mediation

Mediation is about bringing people together and into a position that they all accept. It is a voluntary and confidential process in which people who are involved in conflict with others are helped by a neutral third party to resolve their problems collaboratively (Peaceworks, 2011).

For mediation to be effective, it is important that the mediator never takes sides by preferring one person's argument over another's, and never imposes a solution to the disagreement. Instead, mediation is most effective when the issues that are addressed can be resolved through:

➤ modifying perceptions

➤ modifying behaviour

➤ modifying attitudes (SCIE, 2012).

Mediation can help in a number of circumstances. Health and social care workers are frequently involved with individuals and their families at a time when people feel stressed and face difficult choices. Examples of situations when mediation can help include: family disagreements over making advance decisions about the future care of a loved one; end-of-life planning; and financial and estate planning where a family member no longer has capacity to decide for himself or herself what happens to property.

However, there are occasions when mediation is unsuitable. These include cases where:

➤ the conflicting parties are unwilling to take part in mediation

➤ there is strong disagreement over facts or outlook

➤ there are significant power imbalances, such as with a dominant parent

➤ there are direct criminal law implications (SCIE, 2012).

Summary

Mediation is a voluntary and confidential process in which people who are involved in conflict with others are helped by a neutral third party to resolve their problems collaboratively. It is effective where perceptions, behaviour or attitudes can be modified, but is not always a suitable approach to take.

References

Peaceworks (2011), 'What is mediation?', http://www.peaceworks.org.uk/what-is-mediation/ (accessed 31 January 2013)

SCIE (2012), *Safeguarding Adults: Mediation and family group conferences*, Social Care Institute for Excellence, http://www.scie.org.uk/publications/ataglance/ataglance62.pdf (accessed 31 January 2013)

The medical model

The medical model has been described as the dominant approach to care, and it is one that continues to play a significant role in health-care practice. It is based on science and provides a distinctive way of understanding our bodies when we have an illness or disease. It is an integral part of Western culture and in many cases an efficient and effective method of delivering health care.

What is the medical model?

The medical model views disease or illness in the body as having a specific cause, and considers that removal of the cause of the disease or illness will result in a return to health (Wade and Halligan, 2004). Underlying the model is the belief that disease or illness can be cured by medical treatment.

While it is important to recognise the strengths of the medical model, as it has produced many treatments and advances in health care, certain limitations also need to be acknowledged:

➤ The focus of the model is on the individual's bodily symptoms and the origins of the disease, rather than on all the other factors that could have contributed to the illness or disease.

➤ Too much emphasis is placed on what is normal, therefore making judgements about what is not normal.

➤ The model fails to consider the whole person and needs to encompass a more holistic way of viewing a person's illness or disease.

Summary

The medical model views disease or illness in the body as having a specific cause, and considers that removal of the cause of the disease or illness will result in a return to health. The role that the medical model has played in health-care practice should not be underestimated. There is a need for the model to incorporate a more holistic approach that considers the whole person's needs rather than just a malfunctioning part of the body that requires attention.

References

Wade, D. and Halligan, P. (2004), 'Do biomedical models of illness make for good healthcare systems?', *British Medical Journal*, 329, 1398–1401

Medication

A key treatment for many of the conditions and illnesses that people live with is medication. For some workers in health and social care, management of medication is an important part of their job.

Managing medication

Medication is a chemical substance used as a medicine to cure, treat or prevent disease. The EEC (1965) defines medicines as any substance or combination of substances for treating or preventing disease or with a view to making a medical diagnosis or to restoring, correcting or modifying physiological functions.

To look after people in health and social care safely, workers need to understand the medication that individuals receive. This means being aware of:

➤ common types of medicines used

➤ why they are prescribed

➤ the risks and benefits of each medicine.

The law dictates what workers in health and social care settings should do in respect of medication and what they should not do. The Medicines Act (1968) governs the manufacture and supply of medicines and divides medication into three categories:

1. prescription-only medicines (POMs) such as antibiotics, which are prescribed by a doctor

2. pharmacy medicines such as hay-fever remedies, which can be bought at a pharmacist's

3. General Sales List medicines, such as common painkillers, which can be bought at any shop.

A fourth category, controlled drugs (such as barbiturates), is governed by the Misuse of Drugs Act (1971) to prevent their non-medical use.

Policies and procedures in health and care settings must be based on the law in order to:

➤ contribute to patient safety

➤ ensure appropriate treatment is given

➤ differentiate between different types of medication

➤ ensure medicines are stored safely and securely.

Professional organisations also stipulate how their members should manage medication. For example, the NMC (2008) sets standards for nurses who manage medication, stating that the administering of medicines requires thought and the exercise of professional judgement.

Most medication will be prescribed by a doctor and dispensed by a pharmacist. Care workers also have their roles and responsibilities, which might include:

➤ ensuring the medicine is available

➤ storing the medicine safely

➤ administering the medicine in the correct dose and by the correct route and methods

➤ observing for reactions

➤ disposing of any residual material or equipment

➤ recording the use of medication

➤ monitoring the individual's condition or health status.

Summary

Medication is a chemical substance used as a medicine to cure, treat or prevent disease. All medication used in the UK is governed by law. Workers in health and social care have vital roles in respect of medication.

References

EEC (1965), *Council Directive 65/65/EEC of 26 January 1965 on the Approximation of Provisions Laid Down by Law, Regulation or Administrative Action Relating to Medicinal Products*, Brussels, Council of the European Economic Community

NMC (2008), *Standards for Medicines Management*, London, Nursing and Midwifery Council

Mental capacity

Most people can make decisions about things that affect them in their everyday lives; what to wear, where to shop, what to have for dinner, for example. When people can make these decisions it is known as mental capacity. However, for some individuals their ability to make decisions is impaired by illness or another condition. They therefore lack mental capacity.

What is mental capacity?

Concerns about mental capacity usually affect certain groups of people because they have:

➤ dementia

➤ a cardiovascular accident (stroke)

➤ a learning disability

➤ mental health problems

➤ a brain injury.

The Mental Capacity Act (2005) is the main legislation that governs how capacity is assessed and what individuals and agencies can do. In particular, the Act states that it does not matter whether the impairment or disturbance is permanent or temporary, but it cannot be established solely because of the individual's:

➤ age or appearance

➤ condition or behaviour that might lead others to make unjustified assumptions about their capacity.

Lack of capacity means that individuals are unable to:

1. understand the information relevant to the decision they are making

2. retain that information

3. use or weigh that information as part of the process of making the decision, or

4. communicate their decision by any means.

If it is concluded that a decision should be made for an individual because he or she lacks capacity, that decision must be made in the person's best interests. Consideration must also be given as to whether another way of making the decision is available, one that might not affect the person's rights and freedom of action so much. This is known as the 'least restrictive alternative' principle, and is an important idea that a relative or carer needs to consider (NHS Choices, 2012).

Summary

Some individuals who have dementia, a learning disability, a mental health problem, a stroke or a brain injury have their ability to make decisions impaired. They are said to lack mental capacity.

The Mental Capacity Act is the main legislation that governs how capacity is assessed, and what individuals and agencies can do. The 'least restrictive alternative' principle applies so that the individual's best interest is taken into account.

References

Mental Capacity Act 2005 (c. 9), London, The Stationery Office

NHS Choices (2012), 'Managing someone's legal affairs: Mental Capacity Act', http://www.nhs.uk/CarersDirect/moneyandlegal/legal/Pages/MentalCapacityAct.aspx/ (accessed 31 January 2013)

Mental health

While many people agree on what mental illness is, and there are legal processes that must be followed if individuals have a type of mental illness that puts them or others at risk, pinning down what mental health means is a contested area.

What is mental health?

A simple definition of mental health is the absence of mental illness. This is a negative view of mental health, as it does not add any positive criteria that help in describing an individual who has good mental health. Coombes (1998) suggested that mental health is a state of psychological wellbeing, and therefore is more than just the absence of mental illness.

The Health Education Authority (1997) added further criteria about a positive sense of wellbeing; mental health is the emotional and spiritual resilience that enables people to enjoy life and to survive pain, disappointment and sadness.

However, recalling that the idea of mental health is a contested area, the Mental Health Foundation asserts that being mentally healthy doesn't mean only that you don't have a mental health problem. It campaigns for public mental health in areas such as those connected to fear, anger, loneliness and sleep. For the Foundation, good mental health is:

➤ making the most of your potential

➤ coping with life

➤ playing a full part in your family, workplace, community and among friends (Mental Health Foundation, undated).

It is important to remember that mental health fluctuates. People do not always stay the same. Their mental health can change as their circumstances change, and as they move through different stages of life.

Summary

Mental health is a contested area, but involves more than the absence of a mental illness. It is a positive sense of wellbeing in which people make the most of their potential and play a full part in life.

References

Coombes, L. (1998), 'Mental health' in Chadwick, R. (ed.), *Encyclopedia of Applied Ethics*, vol. 3, San Diego, Academic Press, 197–212

Health Education Authority (1997), *Mental Health Promotion: A quality framework*, London, Health Education Authority

Mental Health Foundation (undated), 'What is mental health?', http://www.mentalhealth.org.uk/help-information/an-introduction-to-mental-health/what-is-mental-health/ (accessed 31 January 2013)

Mental illness

There are many ways of describing mental illness: mental ill-health, mental health problems and mental distress are a few of the phrases used. However, the term mental illness itself is highly controversial. Like the term mental health, mental illness is a contested area with diverse understandings and perspectives among different people.

What is mental illness?

A mental illness causes major changes in a person's thinking, emotional state and behaviour, and disrupts the person's ability to work and maintain personal relationships (PHA, undated). The problems associated with mental illness also affect how individuals interact with others around them and with the wider community. People with a mental illness often find that they are socially excluded from the normal activities and resources that other people use, because of stigma and discrimination against them.

In psychiatry, there are two main ways to classify mental illness:

➤ the *Diagnostic and Statistical Manual of Mental Disorders* (APA, 1994)

➤ the *International Classification of Diseases* (WHO, 2010).

They broadly agree on the main types of mental illness, outlined below:

➤ **Mood disorders**: Depression is a mood disorder in which the individual is sad, loses interest in life, and experiences sleep and appetite changes. Mania occurs when an individual is overactive and overexcitable. Bipolar disorder is a mood disorder where a person's mood swings from periods of depression to long episodes of overexcitement and overactivity.

➤ **Personality disorders**: A personality disorder means that individuals find it difficult to form proper relationships, and may seem manipulative or harm themselves.

➤ **Anxiety disorders**: Anxiety disorder is an illness where the person is unusually afraid or anxious most of the time. It includes phobias such as agoraphobia – a fear of leaving familiar surroundings.

➤ **Psychotic disorders**: Psychosis refers to a group of serious mental illnesses where individuals lose contact with reality. They might have hallucinations such as hearing voices in their heads, and suffer delusions and thought disorders.

➤ **Substance-related disorders**: Substance-related disorders occur where the person consumes substances such as alcohol or drugs that either worsen mental health problems or cause mental illness.

➤ **Eating disorders**: Eating disorders involve a person either eating too little, such as with anorexia nervosa, or eating too much, as with bulimia.

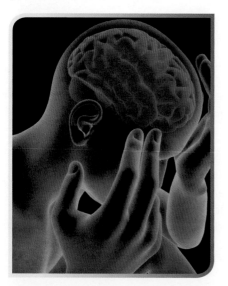

➤ **Cognitive disorders**: Cognitive disorders occur where the person's ability to think is damaged, such as with dementia.

Summary

A mental illness causes major changes in a person's thinking, emotional state and behaviour, and disrupts the person's ability to work and maintain personal relationships. Doctors use two main systems to classify mental illness, but they broadly agree on the main types of mental ill-health.

References

APA (1994), *Diagnostic and Statistical Manual of Mental Disorders*, 4th edition – revised, Washington DC, American Psychiatric Association

PHA (undated), 'What is mental ill-health?', mindingyourhead.info, Public Health Agency, http://www.mindingyourhead.info/home/what-mental-ill-health/ (accessed 5 October 2012)

WHO (2010), *International Statistical Classification of Diseases and Related Health Problems*, 10th Revision, Version 4, World Health Organization

Mobility

Remaining healthy is a significant benefit of being able to move. Without mobility, people can soon become ill through reduced use of the cardiac and respiratory system, and become unfit through loss of muscle tone. There are also psychological and emotional implications of not being able to move.

The importance of mobility

Mobility is the state of being in motion; that is, being able to move physically (*Collins Concise English Dictionary,* 2008). In health and social care it gains importance because sometimes individuals are unable to move themselves or might need assistance with their mobility. They are helped to move by others, who provide support and may also use equipment and appliances that make movement possible. Paralysis or requiring support with mobility can be frightening, and this must be understood when communicating with people you are helping.

Mobility is important because:

➤ it allows people to socialise

➤ it allows people to work, play and keep fit

➤ it affects an individual's independence.

Different health conditions may affect and be affected by mobility. Any disease or condition that requires bed rest or seriously limits activity can be said to affect mobility. Immobility is where movement is constrained. In older people, mobility has been linked to health status and quality of life (Webber *et al*, 2010). The longer a person is immobile, the more difficult regaining mobility becomes.

In health and social care settings, mobility can be affected by problems with joints, including arthritis, torn ligaments, bone fractures, swollen joints and infections. But there are other conditions that restrict movement, such as strokes, depression, dementia, ulceration, muscular dystrophy and spinal cord injury.

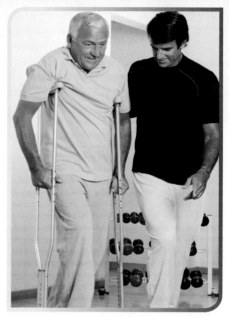

There are several implications of being immobile:

➤ Psychological and emotional effects include loneliness and isolation, leading to depression and anxiety.

➤ Practical and financial effects can result from reduced employment options, and being unable to carry out normal household chores.

➤ Physical effects include muscular and joint stiffness, balance problems and pain.

Summary

Mobility is about being able to move physically, whereas immobility means constraints on movement. It is important for people's health that they are able to socialise and to maintain independence, but in health and social care individuals may need support to move. The effects of immobility include psychological and emotional, practical and financial, and physical effects.

References

Collins Concise English Dictionary (2008), 'Mobility', 7th edition, Glasgow, HarperCollins

Webber, S.C., Porter, M.M. and Menec, V.H. (2010), 'Mobility in older adults: A comprehensive framework', *Gerontologist*, 50 (4), 443–50

Nutrition and hydration

Nutrition and hydration are essential components of health and wellbeing; if neglected, the result can be malnutrition and dehydration. This can contribute to a considerable risk of ill-health (BAPEN, 2009). Over the past decade concern has grown about the nutritional and hydration needs of vulnerable individuals, especially older people, who are being cared for. Health and social care workers play a key role in promoting good nutrition and hydration by making it a priority in their workplace.

What are nutrition and hydration?

Nutrition is normally defined as a source of materials that provide nourishment for the body. A more broad-based definition describes nutrition as a process by which living organisms obtain food and use it for growth, metabolism and repair (*Collins Concise English Dictionary*, 2008). Implicit in discussing nutrition is the need to ensure that every individual consumes a balanced diet. While hydration is defined separately from nutrition, it is a fundamental aspect of nutritional care. Hydration ensures adequate intake of a range of fluids throughout the day.

The National Patient Safety Agency (NPSA, 2009) advocates 10 key characteristics of good nutritional care, which also incorporate the provision of adequate fluids. These are:

➤ delivering food service and nutritional care safely

➤ maintaining an environment conducive to people enjoying their meals and being able to consume food and drinks safely

➤ supporting a multidisciplinary approach to nutritional care and valuing the contribution of staff, service users, carers and volunteers

➤ guidance on food service and nutritional care in service delivery and accountability arrangements

➤ screening all patients and service users to identify malnourishment or risk of malnourishment

➤ designing facilities and services that are centred on the needs of people using them

➤ creating a personal care or support plan for each patient or service user and giving each individual input to identify his or her nutritional care and fluid needs

➤ ensuring staff and volunteers have appropriate skills and competencies and receive regular training

➤ involving patients and service users in planning and monitoring arrangements for food services and drinks provision

➤ creating policies for food service and nutritional care which are centred on the needs of the users.

Summary

Nutrition and hydration are essential components of health and wellbeing, and if neglected can lead to malnutrition and dehydration. It is important to raise awareness and educate health-care practitioners about the need for good nutrition and hydration.

References

BAPEN (2009), *Combating Malnutrition: Recommendations for Action*, Redditch, British Association for Parenteral and Enteral Nutrition

Collins Concise English Dictionary (2008), 'Nutrition', 7th edition, Glasgow, HarperCollins

NPSA (2009), 'Nutrition factsheets', http://www.nrls.npsa.nhs.uk/resources/?entryid45=59865 (accessed 31 January 2013)

Outreach

Some people, while they live in their community, are not really part of it. When they have health and social care needs, outreach helps them to access services.

What is outreach?

Outreach is a way of extending services beyond the normal boundaries of their work to include marginalised groups and individuals. Many varied types of work are carried out by outreach workers. Skills for Care (2009) outlines the role of an outreach worker as being to help people:

➤ overcome difficulties

➤ cope with aspects of everyday life they find hard

➤ develop social relationships

➤ live as independently as possible.

Much of the work of outreach workers is focused on supporting and enabling individuals to live independently and safely as part of the community, rather than giving personal care such as help with washing and dressing. Providing advice and guidance is therefore important. They also work in teams with professionals such as youth offending teams, doctors, social workers, housing officials and the police, drawing on expertise as necessary depending on the individual's needs and circumstances.

Family support workers offer practical help and emotional support to families experiencing various problems, in order to try to keep families together. The primary concern of the family support worker is the care of the children. Problems may include the abuse of drugs or alcohol, one parent in hospital or prison, or financial or marital difficulties.

A community development worker works with individuals, families or whole communities, for example minority cultural groups, to:

➤ empower them

➤ identify their needs and opportunities

➤ plan what they want to achieve and take appropriate action

➤ develop activities and services to improve their lives.

Mental health outreach workers might help people with long-term mental health problems adapt to ordinary life in the community (rather than being in a hospital or hostel).

Summary

Outreach is a way of extending services to marginalised groups and individuals. Outreach workers help people overcome their difficulties, cope with life problems, develop social relationships and live as independently as possible. Some families, marginalised communities and individuals with mental ill-health might benefit from outreach.

References

Skills for Care (2009), 'Career pathway e-tool', Skills for Health, http://careerpathways.skillsforcare.org.uk/what_is/comm/comm_mental.html (accessed 31 January 2013)

Partnership working

Most people are familiar with the idea that interventions in health and social care involve working across organisational and personal boundaries, and within a hierarchical structure where some individual professionals have more influence than others. The concepts of a multi-professional team and inter-professional working imply that no individual practitioner is expected to deliver care in isolation.

What are partnership and collaborative working?

'Partnership' describes the state of a relationship at group, individual or organisational level, and the term tends to be used particularly when formal, cooperative arrangements are being described. Collaboration, on the other hand, is the application of knowledge, skills, values and motives to put partnership into practice (Whittington, 2003). Teams and professional groups are not mentioned, as true partnership and collaboration transcend individual roles and types of practitioners.

The ability to work collaboratively is one of the most important things that social care workers learn. Service users report it is easier to get support where good communication and the sharing of information are valued, and the individual feels like a whole person (IPIAC, 2009).

The Social Care Institute for Excellence encourages partnership working, as it:

➤ is crucial to the provision of seamless social care services

➤ lays the foundations for good quality care provision

➤ involves sharing knowledge about what works in social care (SCIE, undated).

Partnership working cuts across all types of provision including safeguarding adults, working across children's services, and working with individuals who have health as well as social care issues, and housing needs. Partnerships might also be with the police, probation service or other funded body.

Summary

Partnership is about relationships at group, individual or organisational levels; collaboration is the application of knowledge, skills, values and motives to put partnership into practice. They are important concepts because they are crucial in providing a seamless service, good quality care and sharing information about what works.

References

IPIAC (2009), 'eLearning: Interprofessional and inter-agency collaboration', http://www.scie.org.uk/publications/elearning/ipiac/index.asp (accessed 3 December 2012)

SCIE (undated), 'Partnerships', Social Care Institute for Excellence, http://www.scie.org.uk/topic/keyissues/partnerships (accessed 3 December 2012)

Whittington, C. (2003), 'Collaboration and partnership in context' in Weinstein, J., Whittington, C. and Leiba, T. (eds), *Collaboration in Social Work Practice*, London, Jessica Kingsley

Personalisation

Person-centred care, partnerships and active participation are each examples of the ways in which care delivery is being focused on people as individuals, rather than as groups of individuals who may or may not have the same health problems or other conditions. Care delivery is becoming personalised.

What is personalisation?

By personalisation, Carr (2010) means thinking about care and support services in a completely different way. It starts with the person as an individual with strengths, preferences and aspirations. Each person is put at the centre of the process of identifying needs and making choices about how and when they are supported to live their lives. Personalisation means putting people first.

It means that for every individual:

➤ support is tailored to meet individual needs

➤ information, advocacy and advice are available to make informed decisions

➤ there is the means to actively engage with the design and delivery of services

➤ early intervention, re-ablement and prevention are available so that people are supported early on and in a way that's right for them

➤ there is access to universal community services and resources.

For individuals, personalisation can bring about changes to the way they experience care as it encourages independent living and self-directed support. Independent living means:

➤ having choice and control over the assistance and/or equipment needed to go about your daily life

➤ having equal access to housing, transport and mobility, health, work and education and training opportunities (Office for Disability Issues, 2008).

Self-directed support relates to a variety of approaches to personalised social care and achieving independent living. Its characteristics are that:

➤ support is controlled by the individual

➤ the level of support is agreed in a fair, open and flexible way

➤ additional help that is needed to plan, specify and find support should be provided by people who are as close to the individual as possible

➤ individuals should control the financial resources for their support in a way they choose.

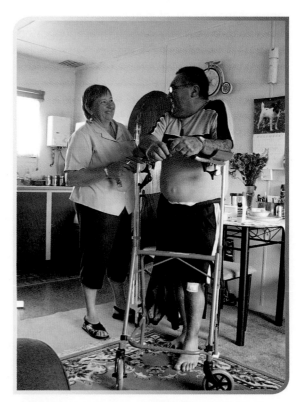

Carr (2010) discusses implications for the way social care is paid for, with the introduction of personal budgets to meet the individual's social care outcomes, and direct payments, which are means-tested cash payments that replace regular social services provision.

Summary

Personalisation means putting individuals at the centre of the process of identifying their needs and making choices about how and when they are supported to live their lives. This approach encourages independent living and self-directed support, paid for by personal budgets and direct payments.

References

Carr, S. (2010), *Personalisation: A rough guide*, revised edition, London, Social Care Institute for Excellence

Office for Disability Issues (2008), *Independent Living: A cross-government strategy about independent living for disabled people*, London, Office for Disability Issues

Person-centred care

There is a growing expectation that when we access a care service, the care we receive will be tailor-made for each of us as individuals. When we go shopping, we make our own choice of goods. In the supermarket, we do not expect to be given exactly the same goods as everyone else regardless of our preferences, our nutritional needs or the amount of money we wish to spend. Likewise, a doctor would not be expected to give each patient the same treatment. In this respect the care we receive is personalised to us.

What is person-centred care?

Person-centred care is an approach that puts individuals at the centre of their own care and involves them in making decisions about matters that affect them (Health Foundation, 2012). It was first adopted as an approach with the White Paper *Valuing People: A new strategy for learning disability for the 21st century* (Department of Health, 2001).

In this White Paper the government set out four key principles, which before long were adopted as good practice in other areas delivering health and social care services as well as in learning disabilities:

➤ civil rights

➤ independence

➤ choice

➤ inclusion.

Talerico *et al* (2003) identify several key components of person-centred care. Care workers should:

➤ know the individual as a person

➤ provide care that is meaningful to individuals in ways that respect their values, preferences and needs

➤ view individuals in care as having biological, psychological and social aspects to their being

➤ foster development of consistent and trusting caregiving relationships

➤ emphasise freedom of choice and reasonable risk-taking.

The overarching purpose of person-centred care is to make positive changes to support individuals so that they can be more in control of their lives, bringing psychological and social benefits. These benefits include gaining confidence, feeling listened to, having self-esteem and feeling valued. Positive social changes might include developing and maintaining new relationships with care workers and others who take a special interest in the individual as a person; and choosing activities that expand the individual's horizons and inclusion in everyday community life.

Approaches to person-centred care can only be successful if delivered by trained, valued and motivated staff. The implication is that care providers must ensure that the way services are staffed and monitored are conducive to person-centred care.

Summary

Person-centred care is an approach that puts individuals at the centre of their own care and involves them in making decisions about matters that affect them. It has key components that promote knowing the individual as more than a care recipient, but is also dependent on the proper preparation of and support for care workers.

References

Department of Health (2001), *Valuing People: A new strategy for learning disability for the 21st century*, Cm 5086, London, The Stationery Office

Health Foundation (2012), 'Person-centred care', http://www.health.org.uk/areas-of-work/topics/person-centred-care (accessed 29 September 2012)

Talerico, K.A., O'Brien, J.A. and Swafford, K.L. (2003), 'Person-centered care: An important approach for 21st century health care', *Journal of Psychosocial Nursing and Mental Health Services*, 41 (11), 12–16

Positive risk enablement

Practitioners know it is vital to manage risks to the individuals they care for, to others in their care settings, and to buildings and property. Managers must compile policies and guidance and ensure they are followed; make sure staff are prepared for and inducted to their roles; and put effective risk-assessment systems in place. However, there is another aspect to risk management that is closely associated with person-centred care and active participation: positive risk enablement.

What is positive risk enablement?

Risk enablement is where dangers to individuals and others are identified, but the support put in place considers acceptable risk (Rowlett, 2009). Positive risk enablement is based on a set of fundamentals outlined by the Department of Health (2010) for people with dementia:

➤ balancing the positive benefits from taking risks against the negative effects of attempting to avoid risk altogether

➤ developing systems for enabling and managing risk that support individuals to retain as much control over their lives as possible

➤ recognising individuals' strengths and building on the abilities that they have retained

➤ identifying less-restrictive alternatives, that is interventions that cause less disruption or change in the circumstances of individuals, but maximise their independence

➤ although agreeing about risk may not be possible, involving everyone in reaching decisions about risk so that they have a shared understanding of the viewpoints of all those who are affected by decisions involving risk.

When decisions about risk enablement are challenging or complex, a risk enablement panel may be convened to facilitate the best outcome. The emphasis is on supporting positive risk-taking while maintaining a duty of care, and decisions are made in a shared and informed way, with transparent, shared responsibility (SCIE, undated).

Summary

Positive risk management or risk enablement is based on a set of fundamentals in which risk is a matter of balancing positive benefits against any negative effects. Risk enablement takes into account maintaining individuals' independence, their strengths and abilities, and is individualised and understood by all who are affected by decisions made about risk.

References

DH (2010), *'Nothing Ventured Nothing Gained': Risk guidance for people with dementia*, Department of Health, London

Rowlett, N. (2009), 'Letting go of the power: Why social care authorities need to start from scratch to deliver choice and control', *Journal of Care Services Management*, 3 (4), 334–56

SCIE (undated), *Enabling Risk, Ensuring Safety: Self-directed support and personal budgets*, SCIE Report 36, Social Care Institute for Excellence, http://www.scie.org.uk/publications/reports/report36/practice/riskenablementpanels.asp (accessed 31 January 2013)

Psychosocial interventions

Traditional treatment in health settings has involved a doctor prescribing medication for a patient. For many illnesses and conditions, this is insufficient and often not appropriate. Instead, psychosocial interventions are used in combination with medication or as an alternative to drug treatment.

What are psychosocial interventions?

Psychosocial interventions are actions health and social care workers can take that focus on psychological and social therapies. They have been used in severe mental health problems such as schizophrenia, depression and anxiety, and cancer, as well as other health-related fields.

The following specific examples are strategies that practitioners can propose to help individuals, and can be used by individuals and others supporting them:

➤ **Dementia**: Moniz-Cook and Manthorpe (2009) argue that psychosocial interventions can be used in the early stages of dementia to help with thinking and memory problems, and psychological and social support.

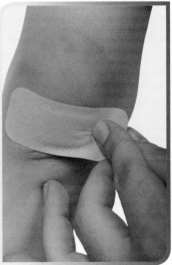

➤ **Substance misuse**: NICE (2007) offers guidance on the role that psychosocial interventions can play in substance misuse. For example, contingency management is a technique designed to change specific behaviours by rewarding positive actions such as abstention from drug-taking, or taking part in health-promoting activities.

➤ **Self-harm**: NICE (2004) suggests interventions for individuals who repeatedly injure themselves deliberately. These include the self-management of superficial injuries using tissue adhesive, such as plasters; harm minimisation techniques such as using clean blades for cutting; and developing coping strategies when in distress.

Summary

Psychosocial interventions are used in combination with medication or as an alternative to drug treatment. They can be employed as self-management and self-help techniques in a range of illnesses and conditions including dementia, substance misuse and self-harm. Others involved with the individual can support with psychosocial interventions.

References

Moniz-Cook, E. and Manthorpe, J. (2009), *Early Psychosocial Interventions in Dementia: Evidence-based practice*, London and Philadelphia, Jessica Kingsley

NICE (2004), *Self-Harm: The short-term physical and psychological management and secondary prevention of self-harm in primary and secondary care*, Clinical Guideline 16, London, National Institute for Health and Clinical Excellence

NICE (2007), *Drug Misuse: Psychosocial interventions*, Clinical Guideline 51, London, National Institute for Health and Clinical Excellence

Public health

Since the middle of the 19th century, many killer diseases have been eradicated in the UK. We no longer fear cholera, smallpox and typhus epidemics. Clean water and sewage systems have played a major role in making our environment safer. Since the second half of the 20th century, other diseases have been the target of scientists, politicians and health professionals: poliomyelitis, for instance, was once common but is now much rarer. This has been the result of public health campaigns.

What is public health?

Public health is about preventing disease and promoting health. Naidoo and Wills (2005) ascribe four functions to public health:

1. an assessment of the health of the population

2. policies to prevent or manage significant disease or health conditions

3. promotion of healthy environments

4. health-promoting living conditions.

While we are now less concerned with killer diseases such as smallpox, public health still has a vital part to play in tackling modern illnesses and their causes: smoking, air pollution, allergies, and mental ill-health (stress and depression in particular).

The public health response to the information age has been to look again at how it assesses the health of the population. 'Public health 2.0' is an example of how modern communication technology and the current policy drivers for engagement and user friendliness have influenced the way data is gathered. 'Public health 2.0' refers to ways that social media can be used by health professionals to interest people in public health (Vance *et al*, 2009). Examples include providing information about public health concerns on social networking sites, blogs and in search engine questions.

Summary

Public health is about preventing disease and promoting health. It has four traditional functions, which are concerned with assessing population health, preventing disease, promoting healthy environments and promoting good living conditions. 'Public health 2.0' uses modern communication technology to communicate information.

References

Naidoo, J. and Wills, J. (2005), *Public Health and Health Promotion: Developing practice*, 2nd edition, London, Baillière Tindall

Vance, K., Howe, W. and Dellavalle, R. (2009), 'Social internet sites as a source of public health information', *Dermatologic Clinics*, 27 (2), 133–36

Quality of life

Quality of life is a significant issue in today's society, but it remains an elusive concept. What makes for a good quality of life for one individual might be unsuitable for another. Personal circumstances, preferences, culture and values each contribute to an individual's ideas on quality of life. However, even though it is difficult to pin down for every individual, there are specific factors such as age, economic status and health that threaten what might constitute an individual's quality of life.

Factors and indicators of quality of life

Common factors that influence quality of life include physical, functional, social and emotional elements. The World Health Organization (WHO, 1997) provides a definition for the concept: individuals' perceptions of their position in life in the context of the culture and value systems in which they live and in relation to their goals, expectations, standards and concerns. Quality of life is perceived as a broad-ranging concept affected in a complex way by a person's physical health, psychological state, level of independence, social relationships and personal beliefs.

In addition to the quality of life at an individual level, there are also indicators – developed by the Audit Commission (2005) – for quality of life at a local community level. These indicators refer to levels of community cohesion and involvement, safety, access to leisure and cultural facilities, education provision, health indicators such as the number of teenage pregnancies and mortality rates, and the environmental conditions in which people live.

While it is possible to undermine the quality of life for individuals and groups of individuals through discrimination and stigmatising practices, it is also within the power of health and social care workers to play a part in improving an individual's quality of life by adapting the way they provide care. For example, care workers can ensure that as far as possible individuals are empowered by:

➤ being given personal choice and control over their everyday activities

➤ being supported in engaging in purposeful employment and recreational activities

➤ being supported in accessing services and personal amenities such as disabled toilets

➤ achieving social integration with local communities, developing friendships, and keeping in touch with families

➤ attaining an acceptable standard of living, with decent accommodation and the personal comforts most people would expect

➤ benefiting from cultural sensitivity to all black and minority ethnic communities.

Summary

While quality of life is something that everyone aspires to, it is difficult to define. It is an elusive concept that is complex and affects people at an individual level and at community levels. However, it is within the power of health and social care workers to play a part in improving an individual's quality of life by adapting the way they deliver care.

References

Audit Commission (2005), 'List of local quality of life indicators', http://www.audit-commission.gov.uk/nationalstudies/localgov/Pages/localqualityoflifeindicators.aspx/ (accessed 19 December 2012)

WHO (1997), 'Measuring quality of life', World Health Organization, http://www.who.int/mental_health/media/68.pdf (accessed 31 January 2013)

Re-ablement

If a person has suffered a stroke or other health condition that limits his or her ability to carry out activities for daily living unsupported, this does not necessarily mean that the individual cannot be helped to regain some of the everyday skills that have been lost. Being helped to become able again is the focus of the type of intervention known as re-ablement.

The importance of re-ablement

Re-ablement has been defined as 'services for people with poor physical or mental health to help them accommodate their illness by learning or relearning the skills necessary for daily living' (CSED, 2007).

The focus of re-ablement is on restoring independent functioning, rather than resolving health-care issues (SCIE, 2012). As such, its aim is to enable people whose health has deteriorated, or those who for other reasons have increased needs for support, to relearn the skills needed to remain as safe and independent as possible in their own homes.

Re-ablement is not intended to be an ongoing provision to deal with long-term conditions or enduring health and social care problems, but aims to be a brief and intensive service in the individual's own home.

Research into users of re-ablement found that they had significant improvements in:

➤ mobility

➤ self-care

➤ ability to carry out their usual activities

➤ pain and anxiety levels

➤ depression (CSED, 2007).

There are three distinct advantages to re-ablement over conventional home care services:

1. greater improvements in physical functioning

2. better health-related quality of life

3. improved social care outcomes.

The re-ablement worker is likely to make more visits to the individual than a home carer, and to stay for longer. A major difference from home care is that the re-ablement worker will do things with the individual and not for the individual. Workers give encouragement or show the person how to do things such as dress, rather than dress the person themselves.

Re-ablement not only serves to help people regain skills they have lost, but is an approach that can prevent individuals from losing skills they already have by:

➤ promoting independence

➤ preventing or delaying deterioration of wellbeing due to age or disability (CSED, 2007).

Summary

Re-ablement focuses on individuals relearning skills lost because of illness or other conditions – skills that are needed to remain as safe and independent as possible in their own homes. It compares favourably to conventional home care and can also prevent deterioration in individuals' health or care needs.

References

CSED (2007), *Homecare Re-ablement Workstream: Discussion document HRA 002*, Care Services Efficiency Delivery Programme, London, Department of Health

SCIE (2012), *Reablement: A guide for families and carers*, London, Social Care Institute for Excellence

Recovery

The concept of recovery has emerged from the mental health field, but it is not only people with mental health problems who face the challenges of recovering from health-related problems. Repper and Perkins (2009) suggest that everyone faces the challenge of recovery at many times in their lives, such as from traumas, physical illness or crises that require a certain amount of readjustment.

What is the process of recovery?

Recovery is not a linear process; it is about growth, development and building a meaningful and satisfying life as defined by the individual, and making an effort to move away from focusing on illness and symptoms towards emphasising strengths and wellness. Repper and Perkins (2009) likened it to a continuing journey where an individual is helped to move forward with support and encouragement, celebrating what he or she has achieved. Rethink, a mental health charitable and campaigning organisation, suggests that there are four key component processes to recovery:

1. finding and maintaining hope

2. the re-establishment of a positive identity

3. finding meaning in life

4. taking responsibility for one's life.

Based on the work of Shepherd *et al* (2008), 10 top tips are suggested which health and social care workers can adopt to facilitate recovery for individuals in their care:

1. Help the person identify and prioritise his or her personal goals for recovery.

2. Demonstrate a belief in the individual's existing strengths.

3. Pay attention to the importance of the individual's goals.

4. Identify networks such as circles of friends and other contacts that are relevant to the achievement of the goals.

5. Encourage self-management of mental health problems.

6. Encourage the individual to suggest the type of therapeutic interventions required.

7. Show respect and encourage partnership working.

8. Enable individuals to talk about other service users whom they admire or who give them hope.

9. Maintain hope and expectations even though there may be setbacks.

10. Embrace new and innovative ways of working.

Summary

Recovery is about growth, development and building a meaningful and satisfying life as defined by the individual, and making an effort to move away from focusing on illness and symptoms towards emphasising strengths and wellness.

Although it has emerged from the mental health field, everyone at some stage in their lives faces the challenge of recovery, whether they are in a crisis situation, experience trauma or contract a particular illness. However, what is important in the recovery process is to have personal goals, maintain hope even when setbacks occur, and be realistic about what is achievable for each individual.

References

Repper, J. and Perkins, R. (2009), 'Recovery and social inclusion' in Callaghan, P., Playle, J. and Cooper, L. (eds), *Mental Health Nursing Skills*, Oxford, Oxford University Press

Rethink (undated), 'What is recovery?', www.rethink.org/living_with_mental_illness/what_is_recovery/ (accessed 31 January 2013)

Shepherd, G., Boardman, J. and Slade, M. (2008), *Making Recovery a Reality*, London, Sainsbury Centre for Mental Health

Reminiscence

Reflecting on the past is a very human pastime and one that is not solely associated with older people. It often involves exchanging memories with the old and young, both family members and friends. Grandparents are often the ones who nostalgically look back, telling their stories to their grandchildren, and sharing their individual experiences of their past lives. A common term used to describe these reflections on the past is reminiscence.

What is reminiscence?

For those with memory problems, reminiscence therapy offers the opportunity to engage with others in a meaningful conversation that improves general wellbeing, self-esteem and a sense of identity. Age UK (2011) refers to reminiscence as a personal collection of memories from the past. Recalling these memories can be highly beneficial to older people, especially those who have dementia. They benefit from being able to talk about their past memories with a relative, carer or practitioner. Reminiscence can create feelings of intimacy and add special meaning to conversations between individuals.

Age UK (2011) suggests the following types of reminiscence activities that can be used as therapy for older people:

➤ simple reminiscence, where the individual is encouraged to reflect on the past in an informative and enjoyable way

➤ evaluative reminiscence, a therapy that may be used, for example, in reviewing the person's life.

Occasionally, unpleasant and stressful information is recalled and this has been called offensive–defensive reminiscence. This can be as a result of behavioural and emotional issues. Dealing with this type of reminiscence can provide a resolution for those coming to terms with a life event.

Obsessive reminiscence occurs when an individual is stuck on specific memories and feels unable to move on. This could result in anxiety, stress, guilt or grief. There is a need to understand the cause of the problem when providing care.

Practitioners can use different triggers to help individuals to remember information that has been forgotten. One-to-one situations are best for engaging individuals in a conversation using triggers such as the following:

➤ visual: photographs, slides, paintings, objects

➤ musical: using familiar tunes from the radio or CDs, or making music using various instruments

➤ smell or taste: using various kits, or different kinds of foods

➤ tactile: touching objects, feeling textures, painting and making pottery.

Summary

Reminiscence involves a personal collection of memories from the past, and triggering them can be very beneficial for older people, especially individuals with dementia. It can help build self-esteem and a sense of identity and wellbeing.

For those who have memory problems, reminiscence therapy can be a powerful tool to help them engage in a meaningful conversation with others.

References

Age UK (2011), 'Reminiscence and dementia booklets', http://www.ageuk.org.uk/ (accessed 21 December 2012)

Resilience

As individuals learn to deal with the stresses and strains of modern living, they develop the ability to cope with the challenges that they face in their daily lives. They discover new ways of coping that enable them to have some control over what is happening to them: they become resilient. Building resilience can lead to better outcomes for individuals in health and social care, where individuals are supported to overcome adversity. Not everyone is resilient, however.

Developing resilience

Resilience is defined as coping with problems or setbacks in one's life. McAllister and Lowe (2011) believe that resilience has been defined in many ways but see it as a person's resistance to stress. They suggest that individuals who are resilient have an ability to cope with adversity and overcome difficult circumstances in their lives. Adapting to adversity is a skill that can be developed and learned.

Children who have been fostered have been the focus of the promotion of resilience. Resilience refers to the qualities that cushion a vulnerable child from the worst effects of adversity and that may help the young person to cope, survive and perhaps thrive in the face of hurt and disadvantage. Some of the difficulties that young people experience upon leaving the care system, such as loneliness, unemployment, debt and problems settling down, can be improved (SCIE, 2004). Skills connected with resilience have also been used in relation to bullying.

The skills and behaviours one can develop in order to become resilient include:

➤ building confidence in oneself

➤ refraining from dwelling on problems or issues that occur in everyday life, but instead thinking of new ways of managing them

➤ taking control of one's life rather than letting events take control

- developing problem-solving skills

- building strong social networks and relationships, so that one has support or a listening ear when needed

- trying to stay calm in difficult situations and always looking for solutions

- building on strengths and using skills when faced with certain challenges.

"He puts a positive spin on everything."

Summary

Resilience is about coping with problems or setbacks in one's life. Some individuals are better able to cope with challenging and difficult situations than others, and are considered to be resilient. Individuals can be supported in developing resilience, and for children leaving the care system problems such as loneliness, unemployment, debt and issues connected with settling down can be improved.

References

McAllister, M. and Lowe, J. (2011), *The Resilient Nurse: Empowering your practice*, New York, Springer

SCIE (2004), *Promoting Resilience in Fostered and Other Children*, SCIE Guide 6, London, Social Care Institute for Excellence

Respect

We all want to be treated with respect, and the term has become a watchword for consideration of the sensitivities of others, and for demonstrating awareness of diversity. The demand for respect is not relevant only to workers in health and social care, but is important throughout society today.

Promoting respect

Respect for other people is about esteeming them for their own personal characteristics. It is linked to dignity; to treat someone with dignity is to treat them in a way that is respectful of them as valued individuals. A person will not be treated with dignity without first being treated with respect.

In mental health services, one of the quality standards requires that service users and their families should be treated with empathy, dignity and respect (NICE, 2011). The majority of participants in the Community Mental Health Survey (CQC, 2012) said they were treated with respect and dignity and were listened to carefully, with only two per cent saying they were not treated with respect and dignity. This positive outcome is achieved through enacting particular ways of working that respect individuals.

Dignity in Care (SCIE, 2010) discusses the following ways of working that promote respect:

➤ enabling individuals to have control and make choices

➤ communicating respectfully and listening to what individuals have to say

➤ providing meal choices and support with eating if necessary

➤ providing pain management to reduce suffering

➤ enabling individuals to maintain their personal hygiene

> enabling people to be independent

> respecting individuals' personal space

> supporting people to keep in touch with friends and family.

Summary

Respect for other people is about esteeming them for their own personal characteristics. Respect is linked to dignity, with particular ways of working that can promote respect.

References

CQC (2012), *Community Mental Health Survey 2012*, NHS Patient Survey Programme, London, Care Quality Commission

NICE (2011), *Empathy, Dignity and Respect*, London, National Institute for Health and Clinical Excellence

SCIE (2010), *Dignity in Care*, SCIE Guide 15, London, Social Care Institute for Excellence

Self-care

Many individuals who access health and social care services will require assistance with their activities of daily living at some point. It might be because they have had a scheduled operation, have been injured in an accident or are experiencing a type of dementia. People usually carry out their activities of daily living themselves; these activities, including using the toilet, washing, dressing, and grooming, are also called self-care skills.

What is self-care?

Self-care is about encouraging and empowering people to take care of their own health (Richards, 2012). This definition can be extended to include personal care that has psychological and social benefits. Self-care also encompasses activities that promote wellbeing and prevent the development or worsening of conditions or illnesses.

Skills for Care (2008) describes self-care as the practices undertaken by individuals with the aim of maintaining health and wellbeing and managing their own care needs. It outlines seven common core principles to support self-care, in which there is a shared responsibility between individuals and care workers:

1. Ensure individuals are able to make informed choices to manage their self-care needs.

2. Communicate effectively to enable individuals to assess their needs, to develop, and to gain the confidence to perform self-care.

3. Support and enable individuals to access appropriate information to manage their self-care needs.

4. Support and enable individuals to develop skills in self-care.

5. Support and enable individuals to use technology to support self-care.

6. Advise individuals how to access support networks and participate in the planning, development and evaluation of services.

7. Support and enable risk management and risk-taking to maximise independence and choice.

Self-care is about people taking responsibility for their own health and wellbeing, and is linked to self-management. The difference is that self-management refers more to individuals coping with difficulties such as illness or disability, and making the most of what they have (Skills for Care, 2008).

Summary

Self-care is about encouraging and empowering people to take care of their own health and wellbeing, and managing their own care needs. Skills for Care describes seven common core principles to support self-care which outline shared responsibility for self-care between individuals and care workers.

References

Richards, S. (2012), 'Self care: A nursing essential', *Practice Nurse*, 20 July, 26–30

Skills for Care (2008), *Skills for Health, Skills for Care: Common Core Principles to Support Self Care: A guide to support implementation*, Leeds, Skills for Care

Self-esteem

In health and social care, practitioners often remark that someone's self-esteem has been affected by a certain incident or that an individual has low self-esteem. But what is meant by this term?

High and low self-esteem

Self-esteem is a term used by psychologists as an estimation of an individual's sense of his or her own worth. People with high self-esteem will have a healthy regard for themselves, be able to appreciate their own qualities and recognise and accept the way they are. Those who have low self-esteem are likely to have a devalued impression of their own worth, and be overly critical of themselves.

In the 21st century a lot of work has been carried out to understand self-esteem, particularly to help individuals who have a low regard for themselves. One of the pioneers of this work is Melanie Fennell, who developed a model to explain some of the processes involved in low self-esteem. Fennell (2005) describes low self-esteem as a reflection of central negative beliefs about the self.

According to the model developed by Fennell, low self-esteem begins with an early experience of failing at a task, or being told you are failing. This leads to foundation beliefs that you are incompetent or likely to fail to cope in specific circumstances. When these circumstances or similar ones arise, triggers lead to negative assumptions about the self, often leading to expecting the worst and to anxiety. This creates a vicious circle in which the individual either fails because of anxiety or avoids the situation completely. In either case, the negative sense of failure is reinforced.

Not surprisingly, low self-esteem is linked to poor mental health, but it can be treated through cognitive behavioural approaches, which are types of talking therapies commonly used to treat people with psychological problems.

Summary

Self-esteem is a term that describes individuals' sense of their own value. Individuals with high self-esteem will have a healthy regard for themselves, while someone with low self-esteem is likely to have a devalued impression of his or her own worth. Fennell's model describes the processes involved in acquiring low self-esteem, which is often linked to psychological problems that can be treated by talking therapies.

References

Fennell, M.J.V. (2005), *Low Self-Esteem*, Springer US, Springer eBook

Self-help

Most bookshops have a self-help section where people browse hoping to find tips for a more fulfilling life. In health and social care, self-help can be a valuable resource when faced with a particular impairment or health condition.

What is self-help?

Self-help is more than helping yourself; it is more to do with reciprocal help in which participants help one another. In short, self-help is about mutual support and information sharing. A good example of self-help is the self-help group, many of which can now be accessed online.

Self-help support groups provide a setting in which people who share similar experiences come together to offer practical and emotional support in a reciprocal and mutually beneficial manner (Self Help Nottingham, 2005). By sharing their experiences, members of self-help groups are able to:

➤ offer unique mutual support based on a common experience

➤ share practical information

➤ discuss ways of coping.

Many people find transitions such as bereavement, diagnosis of an illness or long-term medical condition, or loss of job difficult to cope with. For others, self-help groups are a route to change; for example, they can help a person to make lifestyle changes or overcome a harmful habit.

Self-help groups have the potential to:

➤ empower individuals by giving them the means to tackle problems themselves without the need to be dependent on formal services

➤ help people become involved with others, thereby reducing the risk of isolation.

A quick online search of the website http://www.ukselfhelp. info/ will take you to an alphabetical list of hundreds of resources, organisations and groups ranging from Reunite (International Child Abduction Centre) to a group for XXY Syndrome. They can promote and empower self-help, and some have online discussion forums.

Summary

Self-help is about mutual support and information sharing. Self-help groups help individuals cope with transitions in their lives and empower them to make changes or reduce harmful behaviours.

References

Self Help Nottingham (2005), 'What are self help groups?', http://www.selfhelp.org.uk/selfhelpgroups.html/ (accessed 31 January 2013)

http://www.ukselfhelp.info/ (accessed 31 January 2013)

Self-management

Individuals who use health and social care services have specific and sometimes complex needs, especially individuals with long-term conditions such as a severe mental health problem. Today, care and treatment take place mainly in community settings where there is limited contact with care workers and more contact with informal and family caregivers. Most individuals attend to their own self-care, and many can self-manage their condition.

What is self-management?

Self-management involves individuals developing an understanding of how a condition affects their lives and how to cope with symptoms. Self-management is therefore about symptom control. Special exercises, medication or dietary changes might be required to self-manage a condition.

The term 'self-management', however, does not mean that there is no place for professional support, or no role for others in the management of a condition. Corben and Rosen (2005) propose that the individual is a partner in care and seeks support when necessary. The partnership is between the individual and the care worker looking after him or her. It depends on:

➤ good relationships between individuals and care workers

➤ information being available to the individual about the condition, together with guidance about how to use this information

➤ flexibility by care workers in the ways they support self-management.

Self-management cannot be imposed; a care worker cannot tell individuals that they must look after themselves. It is a choice, based on shared decision-making and collaboration between the individual and the care worker. This negotiated approach underpins all good health and social care interventions. Care workers should discuss with individuals:

➤ what their symptoms are and how they affect the individual

➤ how the symptoms can be managed

➤ what the hoped-for outcome is going to be.

It is very important that the individual sets his or her own criteria for deciding whether the outcome of self-management is successful. The self-report by the individual experiencing the symptom is the gold standard (Dodd *et al*, 2001). Objective measures – that is, what others such as a care worker observe or think about the outcome of their actions – do not take into account the individual's experience of symptoms, so the individual should set the criteria by which the effectiveness of self-management techniques is measured. Individuals might not be able to use medical jargon, but can say whether they feel better or not.

The primary implications for care workers, whether they are caring in dementia settings or with children and young people, are that they themselves should:

➤ adopt a positive attitude to the ability of the individual to self-manage the condition

➤ take positive actions to promote self-management through negotiation with the individual

➤ use the gold standard, that is what the individual himself or herself reports about symptom control, as the measure of the outcome of any intervention.

Summary

Self-management means developing an understanding of how individuals' conditions affect their lives and how they cope with symptoms. A prerequisite is that a thorough assessment is made that identifies the presence or absence of symptoms. Promoting self-management should be negotiated, and symptoms should be addressed as distinct problems for positive action.

References

Corben, S. and Rosen, R. (2005), *Self-Management for Long-Term Conditions: Patients' perspectives on the way ahead*, London, King's Fund

Dodd, M., Jansoii, S., Facione, N., Faucett, J., Froelicher, E.S., Humphreys, J., Lee, K., Miaskowski, C., Puntillo, K., Rankin, S. and Taylor, D. (2001), 'Advancing the science of symptom management', *Journal of Advanced Nursing*, 33 (5), 668–76

Sick role

All of us feel 'under the weather' or 'not quite right' some of the time, and have had occasions when we would describe ourselves as being ill. Being ill, we often feel, allows us a certain status and an expectation that we are treated a little differently, even if temporarily.

What is the sick role?

Talcott Parsons (1951) first discussed the concept of the sick role. Not only is the individual physically unwell, but he or she takes on a new social role of being sick. The sick role, according to Parsons, permits the individual particular rights and brings certain responsibilities. These rights are:

➤ The sick person is exempt from everyday social roles.

➤ The sick person is not responsible for his or her condition.

But the sick person also has certain responsibilities:

➤ to try to get well as soon as possible

➤ to seek help to get better.

Shilling (2002) argued that being exempt from normal social functioning is an obligation as well as a right. A good example is the situation of a person with a bad cold remaining away from work. The individual has a right to rest, but also an obligation to prevent the spread of the virus to colleagues. Being ill therefore also has a moral aspect, as it affects how you behave towards others around you.

Summary

When ill, an individual takes on the relevant social role. The sick role affords individuals certain rights: it's not their fault, and they are exempt from ordinary expectations and obligations. The sick role also brings certain responsibilities: to try to get well and to seek help in doing so. There is also a moral aspect to the sick role.

References

Parsons, T. (1951), *The Social System*, Glencoe, Illinois, Free Press

Shilling, C. (2002), 'Culture, the "sick role" and the consumption of health', *British Journal of Sociology*, 53 (4), 621–38

Social exclusion

Individuals and groups of people who are not part of mainstream society tend to have worse health than the general population (DH, 2010). Some groups are particularly vulnerable to poor health. These are individuals who do not have the opportunities and resources that most people are accustomed to accessing: housing, health care and employment are examples. They are socially excluded.

What is social exclusion?

Social exclusion is a term used to describe individuals and groups who are marginalised. They might include:

➤ individuals who leave care

➤ individuals with mental health problems

➤ individuals who are homeless

➤ individuals with learning disabilities

➤ asylum seekers

➤ substance misusers (DH, 2010).

Aldridge *et al* (2011) link social exclusion with poverty, and cite their findings that while education and health have improved in the 21st century, low income has worsened. Statistics convey some of the effects of being socially excluded, and why a more inclusive approach to practice in health and social care is vital. For example, the average age of death for a homeless person is just 40 years, while a person with learning disabilities is over 50 times more likely to die prematurely (DH, 2010).

The Royal College of Nursing has adopted capabilities for inclusive practice (DH *et al*, 2007) which aim to deliver safe, ethical and fair care. An inclusive approach to care aims to alleviate some of the disadvantage that social exclusion brings. Among the principles underpinning this inclusive approach are commitments to diversity, fighting inequalities, promoting recovery, and a person-centred approach that elicits what matters to individuals.

Summary

Social exclusion is a term used to describe the condition of individuals and groups who are marginalised. They have worse health and some are far more likely to die prematurely than the general population. An inclusive approach to health and social care aims to alleviate some of the disadvantage that social exclusion brings.

References

Aldridge, H., Parekh, A., MacInnes, T. and Kenway, P. (2011), *Monitoring Poverty and Social Exclusion*, New Policy Institute, York, Joseph Rowntree Foundation

DH, Care Services Improvement Partnership and National Social Inclusion Programme (2007), *Capabilities for Inclusive Practice*, London, Department of Health

DH (2010), *Inclusion Health: Improving primary care for socially excluded people*, Best Practice Guidance, London, Department of Health

Social model of disability

A wide range of different individuals and groups of individuals can be described as having a disability, from people with learning disabilities to those with sensory loss or a physical impairment. With some, the disability is visible, and for others it is not so evident. Disabled people are usually identified as having a long-term impairment that is physical, intellectual or medical, and restricts their lives. But is their life restricted by the disability itself, or by an environment that does not accommodate their needs?

What is the social model of disability?

The social model of disability claims that disability is caused by the way society is organised, rather than by the individual's difference, impairment or disability. It emphasises the importance of challenging those barriers that prevent disabled people from participating fully in community and family life, mainstream employment opportunities and education. Removing barriers enables disabled people to be more independent and equal in society, with choice and control over their own lives (Scope, 2012). Barriers include the following types:

➤ **Environmental** – the design and layout of buildings, neighbourhoods and communities. While the Disability and Equality Act (2010) sets out disabled people's rights in everyday life and protects individuals from disability discrimination, many individuals continue to experience difficulty using public transport because of, for example, the height of steps.

➤ **Attitudinal** – prejudicial and stereotyping perceptions that people who are not disabled hold about individuals who are, in respect of what they can and cannot do. This can lead to disabled people thinking they cannot do things that they in fact might be able to accomplish in a supportive community.

➤ **Structural** – the way society is organised, with the prevalence of the medical model in which individuals are seen as disabled by their impairments or differences. The medical model seeks to cure or fix these impairments by treatment or through other interventions, looking at what is wrong with the person, creating low expectations and leading to people losing independence, choice and control in their own lives (Scope, 2012).

Disabled people developed the social model of disability because the traditional medical model did not explain their personal experience of disability, or help to develop more inclusive ways of living.

Summary

The social model of disability refutes the view that individuals' lives are restricted by their disability, preferring the argument that disability is caused by the way society is organised, building barriers to people participating fully in society. Environmental, attitudinal and structural barriers are challenged by the social model of disability.

References

HMG (2010), 'Disability and the Equality Act', Directgov, http://www.direct.gov.uk/en/DisabledPeople/RightsAndObligations/DG_4019061/ (accessed 30 August 2012)

Scope (2012), 'The social model of disability', http://www.scope.org.uk/about-us/our-brand/talking-about-disability/social-model-disability (accessed 31 January 2013)

Social networks

Living in a community implies that people feel included and have access to support. While this is not always the case, as some people are isolated and lack support, for many their community is a place where they are included and have access to supportive social networks.

The importance of social networks

Social networks are about the connections that people make; they are sets of relationships between friends, neighbours, family members and work colleagues. They offer a vital source of mutual support.

Phillipson *et al* (2001) pictured social networks diagrammatically; a person's social network is centred on him or her, with those people who are closest in a surrounding inner circle and others who are less important in middle and outer circles. Using a series of circles to map someone's social network makes it possible to see the number of relationships a person has, and the degree of importance of each of the relationships to the person in the centre.

Social networks are an important part of community life; they can:

➤ offer informal care and support to individuals and families

➤ build friendships and mutual support

➤ be called on quickly at a time of need without the delays involved in referral processes to public services

➤ replace or complement more formal types of support from public services.

Summary

Social networks are the connections and sets of relationships people make: between friends, neighbours, family members and work colleagues. They offer a vital source of mutual support and are an important part of community life.

References

Phillipson, C., Bernard, M., Phillips, J. and Ogg, J. (2001), *The Family and Community Life of Older People: Social networks and social support in three urban areas*, London, Routledge

Special needs

The UK is a diverse society, with many ethnic cultures, age groups, and individuals with differing opinions and preferences. It also includes individuals with a wide mix of abilities. Some individuals are referred to as having special needs, which means they have particular requirements.

What is the meaning of special needs?

In the UK, the term 'special needs' usually refers to special educational needs (SEN). These are needs that an individual child has at school, and are different from the educational requirements that a child would normally bring to the school.

Any child with special educational needs can have a statutory assessment, and if necessary a statement of special educational needs. A statement is a description of all the special educational needs of a child, and the resources required to meet those needs. The statement is based on advice gained from a statutory assessment (Mencap, 2011a).

A statutory assessment differs from other types of assessment children receive, such as those at nursery school or when seeing a speech therapist. It is a formal process with strict timescales outlining what can be expected and when things should happen. However, having a statutory assessment does not automatically lead to a statement of special educational needs.

Parents, a school, a health authority or social services can ask for a statutory assessment. Within six weeks, the parents are informed whether the assessment is to be carried out. The local authority will also give information about the parent partnership service, which offers help, support, advice and an opinion.

If the local authority agrees to carry out the statutory assessment, it has 10 weeks to complete it. The child will be assessed by an educational psychologist and the views of key others will be sought, including those of the child. The local authority then has a further 10 weeks to decide whether a statement of special educational needs is required.

A survey by Mencap (2011b) on the current special educational needs system found it might not work for the benefit of the child because:

➤ it is too adversarial

➤ it is difficult to receive SEN support for the child

➤ barriers prevent parents securing support for their child

➤ most parents thought the system needed to change.

Summary

The term 'special needs' refers to special educational needs. Any child with special educational needs can have a statutory assessment and, if necessary, a statement of special educational needs. However, there are criticisms of the system, which claim it does not always work to the benefit of the child.

References

Mencap (2011a), *Statutory Assessments and Statements of Special Educational Needs*, Factsheet, London, Mencap

Mencap (2011b), *Mencap's Consultation Response: 'Support and Aspiration: A new approach to special educational needs and disability'*, London, Mencap

Stereotyping

The process of stereotyping can have a detrimental effect on the experience of receiving health and social care support. Seeing people as stereotypes affects the quality of care they receive as individuals.

What is a stereotype?

A stereotype is a label that is given to a person or group of people and is based on assumptions made about them. For example, a stereotypical label attached to many long-term unemployed people is that they are lazy and work-shy. The assumption is made that they could find work if they wanted to, but they have been labelled as not wanting to work. Another stereotype relevant to health and social care is that all mentally ill people are dangerous. Stereotypes lead people who hold them to ignore important differences between unique individuals (Shah, 1995). This applies whether the stereotype is about religion, ethnicity or other traits.

A common stereotype about people with disabilities is that they are dependent and helpless. This can become a self-fulfilling prophecy, which forces the person into a role that others make for him or her. For example, if a care worker treats individuals with learning disabilities as if they cannot learn anything, that worker would not expect individuals to learn something and so would not try to teach them.

There are some simple steps that can be taken to avoid stereotyping individuals:

1. Consult disabled people about the support they need.

2. Listen to what they say.

3. Treat people as individuals.

4. Keep an open mind.

5. Recognise each person's abilities and what he or she can do.

Summary

Stereotypes are commonly held assumptions about people based on particular characteristics. They are found in health and social care, where disabled people are sometimes stereotyped, but there are actions that care workers can take to avoid stereotyping individuals.

References

Shah, R. (1995), *The Silent Minority: Children with disabilities in Asian families*, London, National Children's Bureau

Stigma

People who use health and social care services are sometimes exposed to prejudices and are treated differently by some members of the public. In effect they are stigmatised.

What is stigma?

A person who is stigmatised is being disapproved of. The stigma is because the person is perceived as being different from others. Erving Goffman, a famous sociologist, defined stigma as the process by which the reaction of others spoils normal identity. By this he means that the individuality of the person is seen as less important than a particular characteristic or trait that he or she possesses.

Goffman (1990) went further and described three forms of stigma against particular groups and individuals; those who are:

1. mentally ill

2. deformed or of undesired differentness

3. associated with another race or religion.

Many individuals who use health and social care services continue to experience stigma. The Mental Health Foundation (undated) asserts, for example, that for people with mental health problems, the social stigma attached to mental ill-health and the discrimination they experience can make their difficulties worse and make it harder to recover. Similarly, people with other disabilities experience stigma. Earle (2003) argues that stigma can change the way disabled people are perceived; the disability is seen first.

Care workers can help to challenge and overcome stigmatising attitudes:

➤ through education and training

➤ by seeing people as individuals, not as a disability

➤ by being positive about individuals in their care.

Summary

Stigma is disapproval of personal characteristics that make an individual different from others. People who use health and social care services, such as individuals who have mental ill-health, experience stigma. There are ways that care workers can help overcome stigmatising attitudes.

References

Earle, S. (2003), 'Disability and stigma: An unequal life', *Speech and Language Therapy in Practice*, 21–2

Goffman, E. (1990), *Stigma: Notes on the management of spoiled identity*, London, Penguin

Mental Health Foundation (undated), 'Stigma and discrimination', http://www.mentalhealth.org.uk/help-information/mental-health-a-z/S/stigma-discrimination/ (accessed 31 January 2013)

Supervision

In health and social care workplaces, skilled and experienced people have the responsibility of overseeing the work of others in order that they meet their organisational, professional and personal objectives (Morrison, 2005). Supervision is the means by which this is carried out. It is an ongoing process and not just an isolated event.

What is effective supervision?

The focus of any supervision is to develop the supervisee's practice in line with the expectations of the employer, service users, carers and legal requirements (Law Commission, 2012). In doing so, it aims to:

➤ protect the public

➤ increase professional accountability

➤ avoid risk

➤ identify workers' continuing professional practice needs.

To ensure that the supervision session is effective, the supervisee would benefit from being prepared for the meeting, and being an active participant in the process. Before the supervision session, workers should therefore think about:

➤ whether work is allocated according to their experience and skill

➤ when practice risks are identified and how they are addressed

➤ whether their record-keeping is of the necessary standard

➤ whether there are any continuing professional development needs

➤ how their workload is managed and service-user outcomes are achieved.

Employers have a duty of care to their staff, which means that supervisors need to be concerned about their supervisee's physical, psychological and social wellbeing (Boorman, 2009). Supervision therefore should be safe and positive, by being:

➤ focused on the supervisee's practice

➤ based on an agreed agenda

➤ free from interruptions

➤ private

➤ supplied with any supporting information available.

While supervision is normally carried out on a one-to-one basis, in private and in confidence, the records about supervision are not confidential. There will be an agreed format for recording supervision. Records should be made in a timely manner and signed, with the content and any decisions agreed and understood by both parties. The records are then filed, with workers having access to their records.

Summary

Supervision develops the supervisee's practice in line with the expectations of the employer, service users, carers and legal requirements. Workers should be prepared for their supervision and take an active part in it. Even though the session is held in private, records are kept.

References

Boorman, S. (2009), *NHS Health and Well-Being*, London, Department of Health

Law Commission (2012), *Regulation of Health Care Professionals, Regulation of Social Care Professionals in England*, London, Law Commission

Morrison, T. (2005), *Staff Supervision in Social Care: Making a real difference for staff and service users*, Brighton, Pavilion

Transitions

All of us have progressed through life and encountered changes that have marked our growth and development: in education, from our first school to our college or university; and in forming relationships, from being a baby who is wholly dependent on others to becoming a mature adult. These are examples of transitions.

Managing transitions

Transitions are changes in people's lives that are often voluntary, expected and planned. They are turning points as individuals take the anticipated journey of growing up: leaving school, getting a job or going to university, and getting married. Transitions are part of everyday life and mark events in individuals' lives. For Mencap, the charitable organisation working for individuals with a learning disability, a transition is the process of planning for the future as people get older (Mencap, undated).

For many, transitions are exciting and offer choices. However, for some people who access health and social care to meet their needs, transitions can be involuntary, unexpected and unplanned. They bring challenges and worry. Transitions can also involve meeting short-term needs, or be a long-term commitment.

Short-term transitions can be planned and expected; for example, arranging to go into hospital for an operation. They might also be unplanned and unexpected; for example, going into hospital following a road traffic accident.

Long-term transitions can also be planned and expected; for example, an older person might arrange to live with relatives. They can also be unplanned and unexpected; for example, in the situation where an individual with severe mental health problems is sectioned for admission and treatment under the Mental Health Act (2007).

Because of the nature of transitions, people often need support to cope and understand the turning point and challenges they are going through. Workers in health and social care can ease the difficulties experienced with transitions by:

➤ providing as much information as possible in a way the individual can understand

➤ giving the opportunity to discuss issues with an independent person such as an advocate

➤ if the individual is leaving home, arranging a preliminary visit to a new place of residence to alleviate some of the anxiety

➤ consulting the individual about what he or she wants

➤ allowing the individual to control as much as possible of what is happening.

Summary

Transitions are turning points in people's lives and are a normal part of growth and everyday life. For individuals in health and social care, there can be short-term transitions or long-term transitions. Health and social care workers can help individuals cope with challenging transitions.

References

Mencap (undated), 'Transition and further education', http://www.mencap.org.uk/all-about-learning-disability/transition-and-further-education?gclid=CMTKuNzEh7ICFcYKfAodeloAew/ (accessed 31 January 2013)

Vulnerability

People who use health and social care services are often described as being vulnerable because they have particular needs that most individuals in the general population do not usually have. Workers in health and social care respond to the care needs of people who are vulnerable.

Who may be vulnerable?

Any child or adult can be vulnerable. In the case of adults, people over the age of 18 are deemed to be vulnerable when they are at a greater than normal risk of abuse (NHS Choices, 2011) and:

➤ in need of community care services because of a disability

➤ unable to take care of themselves

➤ unable to protect themselves against significant harm or exploitation.

This definition requires the individual to have a disability. This can be connected to age or incapacity, a physical health issue, a learning disability, or mental ill-health. It also indicates that the individual is in need of or receives a community service. On the surface this seems to exclude people receiving care in a hospital or a social placement, such as a residential home for older people. However, if such people did live in their own homes they would be deemed in need of community services.

An individual may be vulnerable to:

➤ abuse, perhaps as a result of domestic violence or sexual molestation

➤ exploitation, such as having money stolen or possessions taken away

➤ a worsening health condition, for instance where the judgement of an individual in mental ill-health is affected

➤ a social need, for example isolation after losing a home or job.

While any adult in need of care for an illness or disability is potentially vulnerable, most vulnerable adults are older people – and most are vulnerable in their own homes. This is especially the case where the older person is unwell, frail, confused or unable to keep up with his or her affairs.

Individuals are vulnerable in their own homes if they are:

➤ isolated, with little contact with friends, family or neighbours

➤ experiencing problems with their memory

➤ having communication problems

➤ having a poor relationship with their carer

➤ being cared for by someone who has drug or alcohol problems

➤ dependent on others for financial and emotional support.

Abusers may create a feeling of dependency so that a vulnerable adult has to rely on them. It is alarming that in nearly a third of cases, health or social care staff were recorded as the alleged perpetrator of abuse (HSCIC, 2011).

Summary

Vulnerable adults are individuals over the age of 18 who are in need of care services because of learning difficulties, physical disabilities or mental ill-health. The vulnerability can arise for a number of reasons – abuse, exploitation, ill-health or social isolation – and affects older people more than any other age group. People can be vulnerable in their own homes where they have to rely on a person who abuses or exploits them.

References

HSCIC (2011), *Abuse of Vulnerable Adults in England, 2010–11: Experimental statistics, Provisional report*, Health and Social Care Information Centre, Social Care Statistics

NHS Choices (2011), 'Vulnerable adults', http://www.nhs.uk/CarersDirect/guide/vulnerable-people/Pages/vulnerable-adults.aspx/ (accessed 31 January 2013)

Wellbeing

The term 'wellbeing' has been used increasingly during the 21st century by policy-makers and others to encapsulate different ways of measuring individuals' happiness and overall health. Yet as a concept, it is often taken for granted.

What is wellbeing?

While it is not easy to measure, the state of wellbeing is seen as having the ability to engage in meaningful activities, feeling good and in control, and being resilient to the changes that occur in life. Wellbeing is a general term for what people collectively agree is a dynamic process where an individual is able to respond to difficult circumstances and manage them effectively. The vision of wellbeing goes beyond the World Health Organization definition of health (WHO, 1948). This incorporates the term wellbeing, but in respect of physical, mental and social aspects.

WHO (1984) later defined health to include an individual's ability to realise aspirations and satisfy needs within a changing environment. This more dynamic and broader definition viewed health as having different meanings for people depending on their abilities and circumstances; a person with a physical disability or a chronic condition such as diabetes has a different criterion as his or her health and wellbeing are associated with quality of life rather than with the disability or condition. This definition included the broader concept of holism. Wellbeing is therefore related to a holistic view of health.

The holistic model of wellbeing is another way of defining this concept. It promotes an individualised approach to health in which good health is not only every person's right, but also their personal responsibility. A holistic approach to health and social care is seen as combining all the different aspects of the individual – physical, mental, social and emotional – into a whole or complete picture of care:

➤ Physical wellbeing is normally associated with physical fitness, good diet and nutrition, and rest and recuperation.

➤ Mental wellbeing is more difficult to define as it varies from one individual to another, but it includes having the capacity to understand, think, judge and respond appropriately in a given situation.

➤ Emotional wellbeing is about being able to express thoughts and feelings appropriately. For example, it is normal to feel sad when someone dies, but to commit suicide as a consequence of the death would be considered abnormal.

Summary

Wellbeing is a difficult concept to define because it covers so many different meanings. The way in which individuals view their personal situation will influence their sense of wellbeing. It is considered to be a dynamic and changing process, depending on whether the individual has a disability or a long-term condition.

References

WHO (1948), 'WHO definition of health', World Health Organization, http://www.who.int/about/definition/en/print.html (accessed 31 January 2013)

WHO (1984), 'Society, the Individual, and Medicine', http://www.med. uottawa.ca/sim/data/Health/ (accessed 20 December 2012)

Whistleblowing

Sometimes care goes wrong, there are incidents of poor practice, or organisations do not fulfil their obligations. It is expected that workers in health and social care settings will raise any concerns they might have with their line manager. However, there are occasions when individuals are put at risk and nothing seems to be done about it.

What is whistleblowing?

Whistleblowing policies encourage and enable employees to raise serious concerns within their employing organisation, rather than overlooking a problem or taking their concerns elsewhere.

Care UK (2012), in its whistleblowing policy, adds that workers might be worried about raising such a concern and may think it best to keep it to themselves, perhaps feeling it's none of their business or that it's only a suspicion. If they tell someone, workers might feel that they are disloyal to colleagues, managers or the organisation. Care UK outlines three steps to be followed if a worker identifies poor practice:

➤ **Step 1**: Raise it with the manager or supervisor, either verbally or in writing. If for some reason the worker feels unable to do this, he or she can take Step 2.

➤ **Step 2**: Raise it at a divisional level. This means going to someone who is in authority above the manager. If this is not possible, or if the worker continues to have concerns, he or she should take Step 3.

➤ **Step 3**: Take the matter to Human Resource and Group Managers.

Lancashire County Council is an example of a public service organisation with a published document on whistleblowing. Lancashire County Council (2012) states the intention to:

➤ encourage people to feel confident in raising concerns and to question and act upon concerns about practice

➤ give the whistleblower feedback on any action taken

➤ inform the whistleblower what to do if he or she is not satisfied with the response

➤ offer protection against reprisals or victimisation.

Neither Care UK nor the Lancashire County Council policy suggests going to the press or outside the organisation about concerns over poor practice.

Summary

Whistleblowing is about raising concerns within an organisation about poor practice. Most large organisations will have a whistleblowing policy, which should encourage a stepped approach to raising concerns.

References

Care UK (2012), *Public Concern at Work: Whistleblowing policy*, Version 3, Care UK

Lancashire County Council (2012), 'Whistleblowing policy: Summary', Lancashire County Council, http://www.lancashire.gov.uk/corporate/web/view.asp?siteid=2767&pageid=4261&e=e#access_s/ (accessed 31 January 2013)

Index